SANTIAGO CHILE TRAVEL GUIDE

Your Essential Resource for Exploring Vibrant Culture, Andean Adventures, Culinary Delights, and Urban Excitement with Insider Tips, Stunning Photos & Maps

DIANE F. THOMPSON

COPYRIGHT NOTICE

SANTIOGA TRAVEL MAP

TABLE OF CONTENTS

SANTIAGO CHILE

INTRODUCTION

WELCOME TO SANTIAGO, CHILE

Santiago, the bustling capital of Chile, is a captivating metropolis that seamlessly blends modern sophistication with rich historical charm. Situated amidst the majestic Andes Mountains and the picturesque Mapocho River, Santiago offers an enchanting blend of urban vibrancy and natural splendor. From its sun-kissed plazas and vibrant neighborhoods to its world-class museums and delectable culinary scene, Santiago is a city that promises an unforgettable adventure.

A City Steeped in History

Santiago's history traces back to 1541 when Spanish conquistador Pedro de Valdivia founded the city on the banks of the Mapocho River. Over the centuries, Santiago has evolved into a dynamic cultural hub, bearing witness to pivotal moments in Chilean history. The city's architecture reflects its diverse past, with colonial buildings, grand plazas, and modern skyscrapers standing side by side.

A Cultural Tapestry

Santiago is a melting pot of cultures, a vibrant mosaic of traditions and influences. The city's artistic spirit is evident in its numerous museums, theaters, and art galleries. From the renowned Museo Chileno de Arte

Precolombino to the captivating performances at the Teatro Municipal de Santiago, Santiago's cultural offerings will captivate and inspire.

A Culinary Paradise

Santiago's culinary scene is a symphony of flavors, a delightful fusion of traditional Chilean fare and international influences. Indulge in hearty empanadas filled with savory fillings, savor the comforting warmth of a steaming bowl of pastel de choclo, or delight in the tantalizing aromas of grilled meats at an authentic asado. Santiago's culinary scene is a journey for the palate, offering a taste of the city's rich cultural heritage.

A Gateway to Natural Wonders

Santiago is not only a captivating urban destination but also a gateway to breathtaking natural wonders. Just beyond the city limits, the majestic Andes Mountains rise majestically, offering opportunities for hiking, skiing, and exploring pristine wilderness. The coast, too, beckons with its charming seaside towns, inviting visitors to relax on pristine beaches and enjoy the vibrant coastal atmosphere.

Santiago: A City that Captivates and Enchants

Santiago, Chile, is a city that effortlessly blends urban sophistication with natural splendor. Its rich history, vibrant culture, and delectable cuisine make it a destination that promises an unforgettable experience. From exploring the city's bustling plazas and architectural marvels to venturing into the surrounding natural wonders, Santiago offers a tapestry of experiences that will captivate and enchant visitors from all corners of the globe.

A BRIEF HISTORY OF SANTIAGO

Pre-Columbian Era

The area around present-day Santiago was inhabited by indigenous peoples for thousands of years before the arrival of Spanish conquistadors in the 16th century. The most prominent indigenous group in the region was the Diaguita people, who were known for their agricultural prowess and their skill in crafting pottery and other artifacts.

Spanish Conquest and Colonial Era

In 1541, Spanish conquistador Pedro de Valdivia founded the city of Santiago on the banks of the Mapocho River. The city was named after Saint James the Greater, the patron saint of Spain. Santiago quickly became the administrative center of Spanish colonial Chile and grew into a bustling commercial hub.

Independence and the 19th Century

In 1810, Chile declared its independence from Spain, and Santiago became the capital of the newly independent nation. The city continued to grow and develop throughout the 19th century, and by the end of the century, it was a major port city and a center of commerce and culture.

20th Century and Beyond

The 20th century brought about significant changes to Santiago. The city experienced rapid industrialization and urbanization, and its population grew dramatically. Santiago also played a central role in Chilean politics, and the city was the site of several major political upheavals, including the 1973 coup d'état that brought Augusto Pinochet to power.

In recent decades, Santiago has undergone a period of significant transformation. The city has made strides in improving its infrastructure and public services, and it has become a major center for business, finance, and culture. Santiago is now a modern and cosmopolitan city that is proud of its rich history and culture.

Here are some of the key events in Santiago's history:

- **1541:** Pedro de Valdivia founds Santiago on the banks of the Mapocho River.

- **1810:** Chile declares its independence from Spain.

- **1973:** Augusto Pinochet comes to power in a military coup.

- **1989:** Chile returns to democracy.

- **2010:** Santiago hosts the FIFA World Cup.

Santiago is a dynamic and ever-changing city, and its history is a fascinating story of conquest, independence, and progress. The city is home to a rich cultural heritage, and its people are proud of their city's unique identity. Santiago is a place where the past and the present collide, and it is a city that is sure to captivate visitors from all over the world.

GETTING TO SANTIAGO

Getting to Santiago, Chile is quite easy, as the city is well-connected by air and land transportation. Here's a comprehensive guide on how to reach Santiago:

By Air

The most convenient way to reach Santiago is by air. Santiago's Arturo Merino Benítez International Airport (SCL) is the largest and busiest airport in Chile, handling both domestic and international flights. Major airlines like LATAM Airlines, American Airlines, British Airways, Iberia, and Qatar Airways offer direct flights to Santiago from various cities around the world.

From the United States:

Direct flights to Santiago from major US cities like New York, Los Angeles, Miami, and Atlanta are readily available. The flight duration typically ranges from 10 to 14 hours, depending on the origin city.

From Europe:

Direct flights to Santiago from European hubs like London, Paris, Frankfurt, Madrid, and Amsterdam are also available. The flight duration typically ranges from 13 to 16 hours, depending on the origin city.

From Other Countries:

Santiago has direct flights from major cities in South America, Asia, and Australia. Check with your preferred airline for availability and flight times.

Upon Arrival:

Arturo Merino Benítez International Airport is a modern and well-equipped facility with various transportation options to reach Santiago city center. Here are the most common options:

- **Taxi:** Taxis are readily available outside the terminal buildings. The fare to the city center typically ranges from $30 to $50.

- **Uber:** Uber is also available at the airport. The fare to the city center typically ranges from $25 to $40.

- **Public Bus:** The Centropuerto bus service connects the airport to the city center with stops at major metro stations. The fare is around $3.

By Land

Santiago is also well-connected by land transportation, with regular bus services from major cities in Argentina, Bolivia, and Peru. The journey time can be quite long, but it offers a scenic and affordable way to travel to Santiago.

From Argentina:

Direct bus services from Buenos Aires to Santiago typically take around 20-24 hours. The fare ranges from $50 to $100.

From Bolivia:

Direct bus services from La Paz to Santiago typically take around 24-30 hours. The fare ranges from $80 to $120.

From Peru:

Direct bus services from Lima to Santiago typically take around 36-40 hours. The fare ranges from $100 to $150.

Tips:

- Book your flights or bus tickets in advance, especially during peak seasons, to secure the best deals and availability.

- Familiarize yourself with the visa requirements for your nationality before entering Chile.

- Consider exchanging currency before arriving in Chile to avoid unfavorable exchange rates at the airport.

- Have your accommodation options arranged in advance to ensure a smooth transition upon arrival.

Enjoy your journey to Santiago, Chile!!!

CHAPTER 1: PLANNING YOUR TRIP

WHEN TO GO TO SANTIAGO

Santiago, Chile, can be visited year-round, but the best time to go depends on your preferences for weather and activities. Here's a breakdown of the seasons and what to expect:

Spring (September to November)

- **Pleasant weather:** Spring brings mild temperatures, ranging from the mid-60s to mid-70s Fahrenheit during the day and slightly cooler nights.

- **Blooming flowers:** Santiago's parks and gardens burst into color during spring, making it a picturesque time to visit.

- **Festive atmosphere:** Chile's Independence Day celebrations take place in September, adding a vibrant energy to the city.

Summer (December to February)

- **Warmest weather:** Summer in Santiago is warm and sunny, with average temperatures in the mid-70s to mid-80s Fahrenheit.

- **Beach season:** Summer is the ideal time to enjoy Santiago's coastal towns and beaches, such as Valparaiso and Viña del Mar.

- **Crowds and higher prices:** Summer is the peak tourist season, so expect larger crowds and higher prices for accommodations and activities.

Autumn (March to May)

- **Comfortable temperatures:** Autumn offers mild temperatures, similar to spring, with average temperatures ranging from the mid-60s to mid-70s Fahrenheit.

- **Fall foliage:** The changing leaves and vibrant colors of autumn add a picturesque touch to Santiago's parks and landscapes.

- **Fewer crowds and lower prices:** Autumn is a less crowded and more affordable time to visit Santiago compared to summer.

Winter (June to August)

- **Coolest weather:** Winter in Santiago is cool and rainy, with average temperatures ranging from the mid-40s to mid-50s Fahrenheit.

- **Skiing opportunities:** Winter is the season to enjoy skiing and snowboarding in the Andes Mountains near Santiago.

- **Festive atmosphere:** Christmas and New Year's celebrations bring a festive atmosphere to Santiago during the winter months.

Here's a summary of the best times to visit Santiago based on your preferences:

- For pleasant weather and blooming flowers: Spring (September to November)
- For warm weather and beach activities: Summer (December to February)
- For comfortable temperatures and fewer crowds: Autumn (March to May)
- For skiing opportunities and festive atmosphere: Winter (June to August)

HOW LONG TO STAY IN SANTIAGO

The ideal length of your stay in Santiago depends on your interests and travel style. However, I recommend spending at least 3-4 days to explore the city's vibrant neighborhoods, historical attractions, and culinary delights. Here's a suggested itinerary for a 3-4 day trip to Santiago:

Day 1: City Center Exploration

- o **Morning:** Start your day with a visit to the Plaza de Armas, the heart of Santiago, and admire the Catedral Metropolitana.

- o **Afternoon:** Head to Cerro San Cristóbal for panoramic views of the city and visit the La Chascona, Pablo Neruda's former home.

- o **Evening:** Enjoy a traditional Chilean dinner at a restaurant in the Bellavista neighborhood.

Day 2: Museums and Cultural Immersion

- **Morning:** Immerse yourself in Chilean art and history at the Museo Chileno de Arte Precolombino and the Museo Nacional de Bellas Artes.
- **Afternoon:** Stroll through the Parque Forestal, a beautiful urban oasis, and visit the Palacio de La Moneda, the presidential palace.
- **Evening:** Experience Chilean performing arts at the Teatro Municipal de Santiago or the Gran Teatro Nacional.

Day 3: Culinary Delights and Neighborhood Charm

- **Morning:** Explore the Mercado Central, a bustling market filled with fresh produce and seafood.
- **Afternoon:** Wander through the bohemian streets of the Barrio Bellavista and sample local crafts and street food.
- **Evening:** Indulge in a traditional Chilean asado (barbecue) at a restaurant in the Providencia neighborhood.

Day 4: Day Trips and Excursions

- **Day trip to Valparaíso:** Discover the UNESCO World Heritage city of Valparaíso, known for its colorful houses, steep hills, and artistic spirit.
- **Visit a winery in the Maipo Valley:** Embark on a wine tour and sample the region's renowned wines amidst picturesque vineyards.
- **Explore the Cajón del Maipo:** Embark on a day trip to the Cajón del Maipo, a beautiful mountain area with hiking, biking, and rafting opportunities.

If you have more time, consider extending your stay to explore Santiago's surrounding areas, such as the Andes Mountains, the coastal towns of Viña del Mar and Concón, or the picturesque Isla de Maipo. Remember to book your accommodations and activities in advance, especially during peak seasons.

WHAT TO PACK FOR YOUR TRIP

Packing for a trip to Santiago, Chile, depends on the time of year you're visiting and your planned activities. However, here's a general list of essentials to consider:

Clothing

- Comfortable walking shoes: Santiago has many walkable neighborhoods, so comfortable shoes are a must.

- Layers for temperature variations: Santiago's weather can vary depending on the season and time of day, so pack layers to adjust to changing temperatures.

- Light rain gear: Santiago can experience occasional rain showers, so a lightweight raincoat or poncho is handy.

- Beachwear (optional): If you plan on visiting coastal towns like Valparaíso or Viña del Mar, pack swimwear and sunscreen.

- Sun hat and sunglasses: Protect yourself from the sun's strong rays with a hat and sunglasses.

Toiletries and Essentials

- Toiletries: Pack your usual toiletries, including shampoo, conditioner, soap, and sunscreen.

- Universal adapter: If you're traveling from outside of Chile, pack a universal adapter to plug in your electronic devices.

- Small first-aid kit: Pack a basic first-aid kit with essential medications and bandages for minor ailments.

- Insect repellent: If you're traveling during mosquito season, pack insect repellent.

- Refillable water bottle: Stay hydrated by carrying a refillable water bottle.

Additional Items

- Camera: Capture your Santiago memories with a camera.

- Phrasebook or language learning app: While many people in Santiago speak English, learning some basic Spanish phrases can enhance your experience.

- Local currency: Exchange your currency for Chilean pesos (CLP) before or upon arrival.

- Comfortable travel pillow and blanket: Make your flight or bus journey more comfortable with a pillow and blanket.

- Travel journal: Document your Santiago adventures in a travel journal.

Tips for Packing Efficiently

- Roll your clothes instead of folding to save space.

- Utilize packing cubes to organize your belongings.

- Wear your bulkiest items, like jackets and shoes, during the flight to save luggage space.

- Leave room in your luggage for souvenirs and gifts.

VISAS AND CURRENCY EXCHANGE

Visas

Most visitors from countries participating in the Visa Waiver Program do not need a visa to enter Chile for stays of up to 90 days. Citizens of the United States, Canada, Australia, New Zealand, and most European countries are eligible for the Visa Waiver Program.

If you are not eligible for the Visa Waiver Program, you will need to apply for a visa before entering Chile. You can apply for a visa at the nearest Chilean embassy or consulate in your country of residence.

Currency Exchange

The official currency of Chile is the Chilean peso (CLP). You can exchange currency at banks, currency exchange bureaus, and some hotels. The exchange rate is typically better at banks and currency exchange bureaus.

The current exchange rate is approximately:

- 1 USD = 874 CLP

- 1 EUR = 919 CLP

- 1 GBP = 1085 CLP

You can also use ATMs to withdraw Chilean pesos. However, your bank may charge you a foreign transaction fee.

Here are some additional tips for currency exchange in Santiago:

- Avoid exchanging currency at the airport, as the rates are typically lower.

- Compare exchange rates at different banks and currency exchange bureaus before exchanging money.

- Have your passport ready when exchanging currency.

- Keep your receipts for currency exchange transactions.

TRANSPORTATION IN SANTIAGO

Getting around Santiago is easy and convenient, with a variety of transportation options available to suit your needs and budget. Here's a comprehensive overview of Santiago's transportation system:

Metro

The Santiago Metro is a modern and efficient subway system that serves the city's major neighborhoods and attractions. It operates from 5:00 AM to midnight daily and offers a flat fare of CLP 700 (approximately USD 0.80) per trip. The Metro is a great way to travel around the city quickly and avoid traffic congestion.

Buses

Santiago has an extensive bus network that covers the entire city and its surrounding areas. Buses are a more affordable option than the Metro, with fares ranging from CLP 500 to CLP 1,000 (approximately USD 0.60 to USD 1.20) per trip. However, buses can be slower and more crowded than the Metro.

Taxis

Taxis are readily available throughout Santiago and are a convenient way to get around, especially for short distances. Taxis are metered, and fares start at around CLP 1,500 (approximately USD 1.70) for the first kilometer and increase with distance.

Uber and Cabify

Uber and Cabify are ride-hailing apps that operate in Santiago. They offer a convenient and affordable alternative to traditional taxis. Fares are typically comparable to taxis, and you can pay with your credit card through the app.

Walking and Biking

Santiago is a walkable city, and many of its attractions are within walking distance of each other. If you're feeling more active, you can also rent a bike and explore the city on two wheels.

Tips for Using Public Transportation in Santiago

- **Have exact change ready for buses:** Bus drivers do not carry change, so make sure you have the exact fare ready.

- **Use a Transantiago card for discounts**: Transantiago is a rechargeable card that can be used on both the Metro and buses. It offers discounts on fares and can be purchased at Metro stations and some convenience stores.

- **Be aware of pickpockets:** Pickpocketing can be a problem in crowded areas, so be mindful of your belongings.

- **Learn basic Spanish phrases**: Knowing a few basic Spanish phrases can help you communicate with locals and navigate the transportation system.

With its efficient and affordable transportation options, Santiago is a city that is easy to get around and explore. Whether you choose to use the Metro, buses, taxis, or ride-hailing apps, you'll find that getting around Santiago is a breeze.

ACCOMMODATION OPTIONS IN SANTIAGO

Santiago offers a wide range of accommodation options to suit all budgets and preferences, from budget-friendly hostels to luxurious hotels. Here are some of the best areas to stay in Santiago:

- **Centro:** The historic center of Santiago is a great place to stay if you want to be close to the city's main attractions, such as the Plaza de Armas, the Catedral Metropolitana, and the Palacio de La Moneda. The area is also home to a variety of restaurants, bars, and shops.

- **Bellasvista:** This bohemian neighborhood is known for its vibrant nightlife, colorful houses, and trendy cafes. It's a great place to stay if you want to experience the city's creative and cultural scene.

- **Providencia:** This upscale neighborhood is home to many of Santiago's best restaurants, bars, and shops. It's also a great place to stay if you want to be close to the Parque Forestal, a large park with a lake, gardens, and a zoo.

- **Lastarria:** This charming neighborhood is known for its art galleries, cafes, and antique shops. It's a great place to stay if you want to experience a more relaxed and traditional side of Santiago.

Here are some specific hotel recommendations in each of these areas:

- **Centro:**

  - **Hotel Plaza San Francisco:** This luxurious hotel is located in the heart of the historic center and offers stunning views of the Plaza de Armas.

  - **Bellasvista:**

  - **Hotel Indigo Santiago - Providencia:** This boutique hotel is located in a quiet street in Bellasvista and offers a rooftop terrace with views of the city.

  - **Providencia:**

  - **The Ritz-Carlton Santiago:** This luxurious hotel is located in the upscale neighborhood of Providencia and offers a spa, a fitness center, and a rooftop pool.

  - **Lastarria:**

  - **Hotel Boutique Castillo Rojo:** This charming hotel is located in a converted 19th-century mansion and offers a tranquil courtyard and a rooftop terrace.

No matter where you choose to stay, you're sure to find a hotel that meets your needs and budget. Santiago has a wide variety of accommodation options to choose from, so you're sure to find the perfect place to call home during your visit,

CHAPTER 2: MUST-SEE ATTRACTIONS

IMAGE OF SANTIAGO, CHILE CERRO SAN CRISTOBALOPENS IN A NEW WINDOW

Santiago, the capital of Chile, is a vibrant city with a rich history and culture. It is home to a variety of attractions, from historical landmarks to natural wonders. Here are some of the must-see attractions in Santiago

1. CERRO SAN CRISTÓBAL

Cerro San Cristóbal is a hill that offers panoramic views of Santiago. You can reach the top by taking a funicular or hiking up the trail. At the top, you'll find a statue of the Virgin Mary, a chapel, and a restaurant.

2. PLAZA DE ARMAS

The Plaza de Armas is the heart of Santiago. It is home to the Catedral Metropolitana, the Palacio de La Moneda, and a number of other historical buildings. The plaza is also a popular spot for people-watching and enjoying street performers.

3. LA CHASCONA

La Chascona was the home of Chilean poet Pablo Neruda. It is now a museum that is open to the public. The museum is a fascinating look at Neruda's life and work.

4. PALACIO DE LA MONEDA

The Palacio de La Moneda is the presidential palace of Chile. It is a beautiful building that is open to the public for tours.

5. MUSEO CHILENO DE ARTE PRECOLOMBINO

The Museo Chileno de Arte Precolombino is a museum of pre-Columbian art. It houses a collection of over 10,000 artifacts from across the Americas.

6. MERCADO CENTRAL

The Mercado Central is a bustling market that is a great place to experience Chilean culture. You can find everything from fresh produce and seafood to souvenirs and handicrafts at the Mercado Central.

7. BARRIO BELLAVISTA

Barrio Bellavista is a bohemian neighborhood that is known for its nightlife, art galleries, and cafes. It is a great place to experience the creative and cultural scene of Santiago.

8. PARQUE FORESTAL

The Parque Forestal is a large park in Santiago that is a great place to relax and enjoy the outdoors. The park has a lake, gardens, a zoo, and a number of walking and biking trails.

9. CAJÓN DEL MAIPO

Cajón del Maipo is a mountain resort area located about an hour from Santiago. It is a great place to go hiking, biking, rafting, and fishing.

10. VALPARAÍSO

Valparaíso is a UNESCO World Heritage city located about an hour and a half from Santiago. It is a colorful and charming city with a rich history and culture.

These are just a few of the many must-see attractions in Santiago. With its rich history, vibrant culture, and beautiful natural surroundings, Santiago is a city that has something to offer everyone.

PLAZA DE ARMAS: THE HEART OF SANTIAGO

Nestled amidst the bustling streets of Santiago, Chile, lies the Plaza de Armas, a vibrant square that serves as the city's historic and social hub. Since its founding in 1541, the plaza has witnessed the unfolding of Santiago's rich tapestry of history, culture, and everyday life.

At the heart of the Plaza de Armas stands the Catedral Metropolitana, a majestic neoclassical structure that dominates the skyline. Its imposing façade, adorned with intricate carvings and towering spires, has stood as a symbol of Santiago's religious heritage for centuries.

Across from the cathedral, the Palacio de La Moneda, the presidential palace, exudes an aura of power and grandeur. Its imposing architecture and well-manicured gardens reflect the significance of the role it plays in Chilean politics.

The plaza itself is a captivating blend of urban energy and tranquil respite. Lush green spaces, adorned with fountains and statues, provide welcome pockets of serenity amidst the city's hustle and bustle. Street performers, artisans, and vendors add to the lively atmosphere, offering a glimpse into Santiago's vibrant cultural scene.

On any given day, the Plaza de Armas is teeming with life. Locals gather to enjoy the warm sunshine, share stories, and soak in the ambiance of their beloved city. Tourists mingle with the locals, cameras in hand, eager to capture the essence of this iconic landmark.

As the sun sets, the plaza transforms into a stage for a captivating spectacle of lights and sounds. The Catedral Metropolitana illuminates the night sky, casting a warm glow over the square. Street performers take center stage, their music and performances filling the air with vibrancy.

The Plaza de Armas is more than just a historical landmark; it is the soul of Santiago, a place where the past, present, and future converge. It is a testament to the city's resilience, adaptability, and enduring spirit. Whether you're seeking a moment of tranquility or an immersion into Santiago's vibrant culture, the Plaza de Armas is a must-visit destination, offering a window into the heart of this captivating city.

CERRO SAN CRISTÓBAL: A PANORAMIC PARADISE

Towering over the bustling city of Santiago, Chile, stands Cerro San Cristóbal, a majestic hill that offers breathtaking panoramic views of the cityscape and beyond. As an emblem of Santiago's natural beauty and cultural significance, Cerro San Cristóbal has captivated visitors for centuries, inviting them to ascend its slopes and witness the city's grandeur from a unique perspective.

The journey to the summit of Cerro San Cristóbal is an adventure in itself. Visitors can opt for a scenic ride on the funicular, a traditional cable car that has been transporting passengers since 1920. The ascent provides a mesmerizing glimpse of the city's layout, with its labyrinth of streets, towering skyscrapers, and verdant parks unfolding beneath the panoramic windows.

Upon reaching the summit, visitors are greeted by a mesmerizing panorama of Santiago. The city stretches out like a living tapestry, with its vibrant neighborhoods, meandering rivers, and the majestic Andes Mountains forming a breathtaking backdrop. The iconic rooftops of the city center, the winding

Mapocho River, and the snow-capped peaks of the Andes provide a feast for the eyes, creating a sense of awe and wonder.

At the summit, a captivating array of attractions awaits. The iconic white statue of the Virgen María, affectionately known as La Virgen de San Cristóbal, stands as a guardian angel overlooking the city. The statue, inaugurated in 1908, is a symbol of faith and devotion for many Chileans, and it offers a serene and contemplative space for visitors.

Surrounding the statue, a picturesque amphitheater provides a stage for cultural events and performances, adding to the lively atmosphere of the summit. Visitors can also explore the Santuario de la Virgen María de la Inmaculada Concepción, a beautiful chapel that offers a tranquil space for reflection and worship.

For those seeking a taste of local cuisine, the restaurant at the summit, La Piojera, offers a delightful menu featuring traditional Chilean dishes and breathtaking views. From the restaurant's terrace, diners can savor their meals while enjoying the panoramic vistas of the city below.

As the sun begins to set, Cerro San Cristóbal transforms into a magical wonderland. The city lights twinkle like a constellation, casting a mesmerizing glow over the landscape. The silhouette of the Andes Mountains, bathed in the hues of the setting sun, creates a breathtaking backdrop, painting an unforgettable scene.

Cerro San Cristóbal is more than just a hill; it is a symbol of Santiago's identity, a place where nature and culture intertwine, and where visitors can experience the city's beauty and spirit from a unique vantage point. Whether you're seeking panoramic vistas, cultural immersion, or a moment of tranquility, Cerro

San Cristóbal offers an unforgettable experience, leaving you with cherished memories of Santiago's captivating charm.

LA MONEDA PALACE: A SYMBOL OF POWER AND RESILIENCE

In the heart of Santiago, Chile, stands La Moneda Palace, an imposing neoclassical structure that has served as the seat of the Chilean government since 1846.

Its grand façade, adorned with intricate columns and sculptures, exudes an aura of power and elegance, reflecting the significance of its role in the country's political landscape.

La Moneda's history is as rich and complex as the nation it represents. Its construction began in 1784, commissioned by the Spanish colonial government to serve as the Royal Mint. Over the centuries, the building has witnessed pivotal moments in Chile's history, including the declaration of independence from Spain in 1818 and the rise and fall of numerous administrations.

In 1973, La Moneda became a focal point of the country's turbulent political upheaval. During the military coup that ousted President Salvador Allende, the palace was subjected to heavy bombardment, its walls scarred by the violence that unfolded. Despite the damage, La Moneda stood as a symbol of resilience, its spirit unbroken.

Today, La Moneda stands as a testament to Chile's enduring democracy. It serves as a vibrant hub of political activity, where government officials, foreign dignitaries, and citizens from all walks of life come together to shape the nation's future.

Visitors to La Moneda can embark on guided tours that delve into the palace's fascinating history and architectural splendor. They can explore the opulent Salón de Banquetes, a grand ballroom adorned with marble floors and crystal chandeliers, and admire the intricate muralwork that adorns the Salón Dorado, the seat of the Chilean cabinet.

The palace's courtyards, once the sites of military clashes, now serve as tranquil spaces for reflection and remembrance. Visitors can stroll through the beautifully landscaped gardens, lined with sculptures and fountains, and pause to contemplate the events that transpired within the palace's walls.

La Moneda Palace is more than just a historical landmark; it is a living embodiment of Chile's democratic spirit. It stands as a reminder of the country's resilience, its commitment to freedom, and its unwavering belief in the power of democracy. A visit to La Moneda is an essential part of understanding Chile's rich history and its journey towards a brighter future.

CATEDRAL METROPOLITANA

Soaring majestically over the heart of Santiago, Chile, the Catedral Metropolitana stands as a beacon of faith and a symbol of the city's rich cultural heritage. This neoclassical masterpiece, officially known as the Catedral Metropolitana de Santiago de Chile, has been the seat of the Archbishopric of

Santiago since 1846, serving as the spiritual center of the Chilean Catholic Church.

Construction of the Catedral Metropolitana began in 1743, replacing an earlier wooden structure that was destroyed by an earthquake. The project spanned over a century, with the final touches being added in 1880. The cathedral's design is attributed to Italian architect Toesca, who drew inspiration from European cathedrals, blending neoclassical elements with local architectural traditions.

The Catedral Metropolitana's imposing façade, adorned with intricate carvings and towering spires, dominates the Plaza de Armas, the city's central square. Its grand entrance, framed by Corinthian columns, leads into a vast interior that leaves visitors awestruck. The cathedral's nave, with its soaring vaulted ceilings and stained-glass windows, creates an atmosphere of awe and reverence.

The cathedral's interior is a treasure trove of artistic and historical significance. The main altar, a masterpiece of Chilean craftsmanship, is adorned with gold and marble, while the pulpit, carved from a single block of wood, is a testament to the skill of local artisans. The cathedral also houses a collection of relics, including a piece of the True Cross and a fragment of the veil worn by the Virgin Mary.

Beyond its religious significance, the Catedral Metropolitana is a cherished landmark that holds a special place in the hearts of Chileans. It has witnessed countless baptisms, weddings, and funerals, serving as a backdrop for the city's most important life events. The cathedral has also been a focal point for social and political gatherings, hosting events that have shaped Chile's history.

Today, the Catedral Metropolitana remains a vibrant center of faith and community. Daily masses and special ceremonies draw visitors from all corners of Santiago, while tourists flock to admire its architectural splendor and immerse themselves in its rich history. The cathedral also serves as a hub for social outreach programs, providing support and assistance to those in need.

The Catedral Metropolitana is more than just a building; it is an embodiment of Santiago's spirit, a symbol of its faith, and a testament to its enduring heritage. A visit to this iconic landmark is an essential part of understanding the city's soul and its place in Chilean history.

MERCADO CENTRAL: A CULINARY ADVENTURE IN SANTIAGO

In the heart of Santiago, Chile, amidst the vibrant streets and bustling energy of the city, lies the Mercado Central, a culinary paradise that delights the senses and captures the essence of Chilean cuisine. This historic market, dating back to the late 19th century, is a symphony of flavors,

This historic market, dating back to the late 19th century, is a symphony of flavors, aromas, and sights, offering an immersive experience into the country's rich gastronomic heritage.

Stepping into the Mercado Central is like stepping into a world of culinary delights. The air is thick with the enticing aroma of fresh produce, seafood, and spices, enticing visitors to explore the market's vast array of treasures. Stalls overflow with colorful fruits and vegetables, their vibrant hues painting a picturesque scene. Freshly caught seafood, glistening with ocean freshness, beckons from ice-filled displays, while the tantalizing aroma of roasting meats and sizzling seafood wafts through the air.

The Mercado Central is a haven for seafood lovers, offering an abundance of marine delicacies from the Chilean coast. Octopus, squid, shrimp, and a variety of fish, from tuna to salmon, await, ready to be transformed into culinary masterpieces. Local vendors eagerly showcase their catches, sharing stories of their fishing expeditions and the freshness of their products.

Beyond seafood, the Mercado Central offers a diverse array of Chilean specialties. Empanadas, savory pastries filled with a variety of fillings, from cheese and meat to seafood and vegetables, are a must-try. Pastel de choclo, a hearty corn casserole, is a comforting dish that embodies traditional Chilean flavors. And for those seeking a sweet indulgence, alfajores, melt-in-your-mouth cookies filled with dulce de leche, are a delightful treat.

The Mercado Central is not just a place to buy ingredients; it's a place to experience the vibrant culture of Santiago. Local chefs and artisans showcase their culinary skills, preparing dishes right before your eyes. The market's lively atmosphere is infectious, filled with the chatter of vendors, the laughter of customers, and the rhythmic chopping of knives.

Whether you're a seasoned foodie or a curious traveler seeking a taste of authentic Chilean cuisine, the Mercado Central is an unforgettable culinary adventure. Let your senses guide you as you explore the market's labyrinthine aisles, savor the flavors of Chile, and immerse yourself in the vibrant heart of Santiago.

BARRIO BELLAVISTA: A BOHEMIAN RHAPSODY IN SANTIAGO

Nestled amidst the bustling streets of Santiago, Chile, lies Barrio Bellavista, a bohemian haven that pulsates with creativity, vibrancy, and a touch of eccentricity. This enchanting neighborhood, known for its colorful houses, trendy bars, and artistic spirit, has long been a magnet for artists, musicians, and freethinkers seeking inspiration and camaraderie.

As you wander through the cobblestone streets of Barrio Bellavista, you'll be captivated by the kaleidoscope of colors adorning the walls of its houses. Murals depicting scenes from Chilean history and folklore intertwine with graffiti tags, creating a mesmerizing tapestry of urban art. The neighborhood's architectural charm is further enhanced by its eclectic mix of Spanish colonial buildings, Art Deco structures, and modern apartments.

Barrio Bellavista is not just a feast for the eyes; it's a symphony of sounds that will entice and entertain. The air is filled with the rhythmic beats of salsa, the soulful melodies of Chilean folk music, and the electrifying energy of rock and roll bands. Music venues ranging from intimate cafes to open-air plazas showcase the neighborhood's vibrant music scene, providing a stage for local talent and international acts alike.

When the sun dips below the horizon, Barrio Bellavista transforms into a nocturnal wonderland. Trendy bars and lively pubs spill onto the streets, their neon lights casting an inviting glow. The neighborhood's bohemian spirit comes alive under the cloak of night, as locals and visitors mingle, enjoying lively conversations and indulging in delectable cocktails.

Art galleries and cultural centers scattered throughout Barrio Bellavista provide a window into the neighborhood's creative soul. Exhibitions showcasing the works of local artists, from painters and sculptors to photographers and filmmakers, inspire and engage visitors. Theater performances and poetry readings add to the neighborhood's cultural tapestry, offering thought-provoking experiences and artistic expressions.

Barrio Bellavista is more than just a neighborhood; it's a living embodiment of Santiago's artistic spirit and bohemian lifestyle. It's a place where creativity flourishes, where individuality is celebrated, and where the night comes alive with the rhythm of music and the energy of free expression. Whether you're seeking artistic inspiration, a taste of Santiago's nightlife, or simply a place to let loose and immerse yourself in the city's vibrant culture, Barrio Bellavista is an unforgettable destination.

PROVIDENCIA: A TRENDY DISTRICT WITH UPSCALE SHOPS AND RESTAURANTS

Providencia is a trendy district in Santiago, Chile, known for its upscale shops, restaurants, and nightlife. It is a popular destination for both locals and tourists alike.

Here are some of the things you can do in Providencia:

- **Shop at the many upscale boutiques and malls.** Providencia is home to some of the best shopping in Santiago, with everything from high-end designer brands to local boutiques.

- **Dine at one of the many excellent restaurants.** Providencia has a wide variety of restaurants to choose from, including fine dining, casual eateries, and everything in between.

- **Enjoy the nightlife.** Providencia is home to some of the best bars and clubs in Santiago.

- **Visit one of the many parks.** Providencia has a number of parks, perfect for a relaxing stroll or picnic.

Here are some of the most popular attractions in Providencia:

- **Costanera Center:** This is the largest shopping mall in South America, with over 600 stores and restaurants.

- **Parque Bicentenario:** This is a large park with a lake, gardens, and a children's playground.

- **Patio Bellavista:** This is a popular nightlife spot with a variety of bars and restaurants.

- **Parque Forestal:** This is a large park with a lake, gardens, and a zoo.

Providencia is a great place to stay if you want to be in the heart of the action. There are a number of hotels to choose from, in all price ranges.

Here are some of the most popular hotels in Providencia:

- **Hotel W Santiago:** This is a luxury hotel with a rooftop bar and pool.

- **The Ritz-Carlton, Santiago:** This is another luxury hotel with a spa and fitness center.

- **Hotel Indigo Santiago - Providencia:** This is a boutique hotel with a rooftop terrace.

- **Hotel Courtyard by Marriott Santiago Providencia:** This is a business-friendly hotel with a conference center.

If you are looking for a trendy and upscale district to stay in Santiago, Providencia is a great option. With its many shops, restaurants, and nightlife options, you are sure to find something to keep you entertained.

LASTARRIA: A BOHEMIAN CHARM IN SANTIAGO'S HEART

In the heart of Santiago, Chile, nestled amidst the city's vibrant pulse, lies the charming neighborhood of Lastarria, an oasis of bohemian spirit, artistic expression, and captivating history. Once the home of Chile's elite, Lastarria has transformed into a haven for artists, musicians, and free-thinkers, its cobblestone streets echoing with creativity and a touch of eccentricity.

Strolling through Lastarria's labyrinthine lanes, you'll be captivated by its architectural charm, a harmonious blend of 19th-century buildings and contemporary structures. Majestic mansions with ornate facades stand alongside modern art galleries, their contrasting styles creating a captivating visual tapestry. The neighborhood's plazas and courtyards offer tranquil respites, adorned with lush greenery and inviting fountains, providing a welcome escape from the city's bustling energy.

Lastarria is a feast for the eyes, its walls adorned with vibrant murals that depict scenes from Chilean history, folklore, and contemporary art. The neighborhood's artistic spirit extends beyond its murals, with numerous art galleries showcasing the works of local and international artists. From captivating paintings and sculptures to thought-provoking photography and installations, Lastarria's art scene is a vibrant expression of creativity and cultural diversity.

As the sun begins to set, Lastarria transforms into a bohemian wonderland, its streets illuminated by the warm glow of cafes and bars. The air fills with the enticing aroma of freshly brewed coffee and tantalizing dishes, drawing in locals and visitors alike. Cozy cafes tucked away in charming corners offer a perfect setting for leisurely conversations and indulging in the neighborhood's delightful culinary creations.

Lastarria's nightlife is an electrifying blend of traditional Chilean music, lively salsa beats, and contemporary electronic sounds. Music venues, ranging from intimate cafes to open-air plazas, showcase the neighborhood's vibrant musical scene, providing a stage for local talent and international acts alike. As the night progresses, Lastarria's streets come alive with the rhythm of music and the energy of free expression.

Lastarria is more than just a neighborhood; it's a living embodiment of Santiago's bohemian spirit and artistic soul. It's a place where creativity thrives, where individuality is celebrated, and where the city's history and culture intertwine with a touch of eccentricity. Whether you're seeking artistic inspiration, a taste of Santiago's vibrant nightlife, or simply a place to wander and immerse yourself in the city's captivating charm, Lastarria is an unforgettable destination.

PARQUE FORESTAL: A GREEN OASIS IN SANTIAGO'S HEART

Nestled amidst the bustling cityscape of Santiago, Chile, lies the Parque Forestal, a sprawling urban oasis that offers a welcome respite from the city's vibrant energy. This expansive park, stretching over 7 hectares, is a cherished haven for locals and visitors alike, providing a tranquil escape into nature's embrace.

The park's verdant expanse is a welcome sight amidst the concrete jungle of Santiago. Lush green lawns, adorned with a variety of trees and shrubs, provide ample space for leisurely strolls, picnics, and outdoor activities. The park's meandering pathways, lined with fragrant flowers and shady trees, invite visitors to explore its hidden corners and discover its many treasures.

At the heart of the Parque Forestal lies the glistening lake, a serene oasis that reflects the surrounding greenery and the towering skyscrapers of the city skyline. Visitors can rent paddleboats and glide across the lake's tranquil waters, enjoying a unique perspective of the park's beauty. The lake's shores are lined with benches, providing a perfect spot to relax, soak up the sun, and observe the lively activity surrounding the park.

The Parque Forestal is not just a place for relaxation; it's also a hub for cultural and artistic expression. The park's open-air amphitheater hosts various events throughout the year, from concerts and theatrical performances to art exhibitions and craft fairs. These events bring the park to life, transforming it into a vibrant stage for local talent and cultural expression.

For those seeking a taste of nature's wonders, the Parque Forestal is home to the Zoológico Nacional de Chile, a beloved institution that houses a diverse array of animal species from around the world. Visitors can embark on a journey through the animal kingdom, encountering majestic lions, playful penguins, and a variety of other fascinating creatures. The zoo's educational exhibits provide insights into animal conservation and the importance of preserving our planet's biodiversity.

The Parque Forestal is a testament to the importance of green spaces in urban environments. It provides a vital refuge for wildlife, a haven for recreation and relaxation, and a stage for cultural expression. Whether you're seeking a tranquil escape, a cultural immersion, or simply a place to reconnect with nature, the Parque Forestal is an essential part of Santiago's vibrant tapestry.

CHAPTER 3: CULTURAL EXPERIENCES

S antiago is a vibrant and cosmopolitan city with a rich cultural heritage. Visitors can find a wide variety of cultural experiences to enjoy, from visiting museums and art galleries to attending concerts and theatrical performances.

Museums and Art Galleries

Santiago is home to a number of world-class museums and art galleries, showcasing a wide range of art and artifacts from Chile and around the world. Some of the most popular museums include:

- **Museo Chileno de Arte Precolombino:** This museum houses a vast collection of pre-Columbian art from throughout the Americas, including ceramics, textiles, and jewelry.

- **Museo Nacional de Bellas Artes:** This museum houses a collection of Chilean and international art, including paintings, sculptures, and drawings.

- **Museo de Arte Contemporáneo:** This museum showcases contemporary art from Chile and around the world.

- **Museo de la Memoria y los Derechos Humanos**: This museum commemorates the victims of the Chilean dictatorship of 1973-1990.

Concerts and Theater

Santiago is a major cultural center for Latin America, and it hosts a wide variety of concerts and theatrical performances throughout the year. Some of the most popular venues include:

- **Teatro Municipal de Santiago:** This opera house is one of the most important cultural institutions in Chile.

- **Festival Internacional de Teatro Santiago a Mil:** This annual festival features a wide variety of theatrical performances from around the world.

- **Festival de Música de Santiago:** This annual festival features a wide variety of musical performances from around the world.

Other Cultural Experiences

In addition to museums, art galleries, concerts, and theater, Santiago also offers a variety of other cultural experiences, such as:

- **Visiting the Plaza de Armas:** This central square is the heart of Santiago and is home to a number of important historical buildings, including the Catedral Metropolitana and the Palacio de la Moneda.

- **Taking a walk through the Parque Forestal:** This sprawling park is a popular spot for locals and visitors alike to relax, picnic, and enjoy the outdoors.

- **Learning about Chilean culture:** There are a number of cultural centers in Santiago that offer classes and workshops on Chilean history, culture, and language.

Santiago is a vibrant and cosmopolitan city with a rich cultural heritage. Visitors can find a wide variety of cultural experiences to enjoy, from visiting museums and art galleries to attending concerts and theatrical performances.

MUSEUMS

MUSEO CHILENO DE ARTE PRECOLOMBINO

The Museo Chileno de Arte Precolombino, also known as the Chilean Museum of Pre-Columbian Art, is a museum in Santiago, Chile, dedicated to the study and display of pre-Columbian art and artifacts from Central and South America. The museum was founded by the Chilean architect and antiquities collector Sergio Larraín García-Moreno, who had sought premises for the display and preservation of his private collection of pre-Columbian artefacts acquired over the course of nearly fifty years.

The museum's collection includes over 45,000 objects from a variety of cultures, including the Moche, Inca, Maya, and Aztec. The collection is divided into five main galleries:

- **Galería Andes Centrales:** This gallery showcases art and artifacts from the Central Andes, including ceramics, textiles, and jewelry from the Moche, Nazca, and Inca cultures.

- **Galería Andes Septentrionales:** This gallery showcases art and artifacts from the Northern Andes, including ceramics, textiles, and jewelry from the Chavín, Chimú, and Tairona cultures.

- **Galería Andes Meridionales:** This gallery showcases art and artifacts from the Southern Andes, including ceramics, textiles, and jewelry from the Mapuche, Aymara, and Atacameño cultures.

- **Galería Mesoamérica:** This gallery showcases art and artifacts from Mesoamerica, including ceramics, textiles, and jewelry from the Maya, Olmec, and Aztec cultures.

- **Galería Objetos Especiales:** This gallery showcases a variety of special objects, including goldwork, metalwork, and stonework.

The museum also offers a variety of educational programs, including guided tours, workshops, and lectures. The museum is a popular destination for both locals and tourists, and it is a valuable resource for learning about the rich pre-Columbian cultures of the Americas.

Some of the museum's most notable exhibits include:

- **The Golden Head of Cahuachi:** This Moche gold head is one of the most iconic objects in the museum's collection. It is thought to have been a portrait of a Moche ruler or priest.

- **The Paracas Necropolis Textiles:** These textiles are some of the finest examples of pre-Columbian weaving. They are characterized by their intricate designs and use of vibrant colors.

- **The Chavín Monolithic Head**: This massive stone head is one of the most important archaeological finds in Peru. It is thought to have been a representation of the Chavín god, Wiracocha.

- **The Aztec Calendar Stone:** This massive stone calendar is one of the most iconic objects in Mesoamerican culture. It is thought to have been used for astronomical and religious purposes.

The Museo Chileno de Arte Precolombino is a must-see for anyone interested in learning about the rich and diverse cultures of the Americas.

MUSEO NACIONAL DE BELLAS ARTES

The Museo Nacional de Bellas Artes, also known as the National Museum of Fine Arts, is a museum in Santiago, Chile, dedicated to the collection, preservation, and exhibition of Chilean and international art. The museum was founded in 1880 and is one of the oldest and most important museums in Chile.

The museum's collection includes over 12,000 works of art, including paintings, sculptures, drawings, and prints. The collection is divided into three main periods:

- **Colonial art:** This period includes works from the 16th to the 19th centuries, including religious paintings and sculptures.

- **19th-century art:** This period includes works from the 19th century, including landscape paintings and portraits.

- **20th-century art:** This period includes works from the 20th century, including modern and contemporary art.

The museum's collection includes works by some of the most important Chilean artists, including:

- **José Gil de Castro:** This 19th-century artist is known for his portraits of Chilean leaders and figures.

- **Juan Francisco González:** This 19th-century artist is known for his landscape paintings.

- **Antonio Smith:** This 19th-century artist is known for his portraits of Chilean women.

- **Pedro Lira:** This 19th-century artist is known for his historical paintings.

- **Roberto Matta:** This 20th-century artist is known for his surrealist paintings.

- **Graciela Iturbide:** This 20th-century artist is known for her photographs of Mexican culture.

The museum also hosts a variety of exhibitions, including temporary exhibitions of Chilean and international art, as well as educational programs, such as guided tours, workshops, and lectures. The museum is a popular destination for both locals and tourists, and it is a valuable resource for learning about the history of Chilean art.

Some of the museum's most notable exhibits include:

- **The collection of 19th-century Chilean art:** This collection includes works by some of the most important Chilean artists of the 19th century, such as José Gil de Castro, Juan Francisco González, and Antonio Smith.

- **The collection of Chilean modern and contemporary art:** This collection includes works by some of the most important Chilean artists of the 20th and 21st centuries, such as Pedro Lira, Roberto Matta, and Graciela Iturbide.

- **The collection of international art:** This collection includes works by artists from around the world, including Pablo Picasso, Vincent van Gogh, and Rembrandt.

The Museo Nacional de Bellas Artes is a must-see for anyone interested in learning about the history of Chilean art.

MUSEO HISTÓRICO NACIONAL

Nestled in the heart of Santiago, Chile, the Museo Histórico Nacional, also known as the National Historical Museum, stands as a testament to the country's rich and captivating past. Housed within the majestic Palacio de la Real Audiencia, a 19th-century building that once served as the seat of the Spanish colonial government, the museum invites visitors to embark on an immersive journey through the annals of Chilean history.

From pre-Columbian civilizations to the modern era, the Museo Histórico Nacional's extensive collection encompasses a diverse array of artifacts, documents, and artworks that chronicle Chile's cultural, social, and political evolution. Visitors can trace the footsteps of indigenous peoples, explore the colonial era's transformative impact, and witness the struggles and triumphs that shaped Chile's national identity.

Highlights of the Museum's Collection:

- **Pre-Columbian Artifacts:** Delve into the world of Chile's indigenous inhabitants, encountering exquisite ceramics, intricate textiles, and ceremonial objects that showcase their artistry and craftsmanship.

- **Colonial Era Treasures:** Immerse yourself in the colonial period, exploring furniture, paintings, and religious artifacts that reflect the influence of Spanish culture and the blending of European and indigenous traditions.

- **Independence and Republican Era Exhibits:** Discover the stories of Chile's struggle for independence and the formation of its republic, examining documents, weapons, and personal belongings of key figures who shaped the nation's destiny.

- **20th-Century Transformations:** Explore the social, political, and cultural upheavals of the 20th century, witnessing the rise of democracy, the impact of social movements, and the country's artistic and intellectual expressions.

Educational Programs and Activities:

The Museo Histórico Nacional is not merely a repository of artifacts; it is a dynamic center for learning and engagement. The museum offers a variety of educational programs and activities to enhance visitors' understanding of Chilean history, including:

- Guided Tours: Experienced docents lead visitors through the museum's galleries, providing in-depth insights into the exhibits and historical context.

- Interactive Workshops: Hands-on workshops allow participants to engage with historical materials, recreate ancient crafts, and explore the museum's collection in a participatory manner.

- Educational Seminars and Lectures: Renowned scholars and experts conduct seminars and lectures on various aspects of Chilean history, offering specialized knowledge and fostering intellectual exchange.

The Museo Histórico Nacional stands as an invaluable resource for understanding Chile's rich heritage and the forces that have shaped its unique identity. Through its comprehensive collection, engaging exhibitions, and educational programs, the museum inspires visitors to connect with the past, appreciate the present, and contemplate the future of this dynamic nation.

PERFORMING ARTS

TEATRO MUNICIPAL DE SANTIAGO

Nestled in the heart of Santiago, Chile, the Teatro Municipal de Santiago stands as a magnificent symbol of the city's cultural vibrancy and artistic spirit. This opulent opera house, renowned for its stunning architecture and world-class productions, has captivated audiences for over a century, showcasing a diverse array of performances that span opera, ballet, classical music, and contemporary dance.

The Teatro Municipal de Santiago's rich history dates back to 1857, when construction on the grand structure commenced. The theater's opening night, in 1858, marked a pivotal moment in Chilean culture, ushering in a new era of artistic expression and appreciation. Over the years, the Teatro Municipal de Santiago has hosted performances by renowned international artists, further cementing its status as a premier cultural institution.

The Teatro Municipal de Santiago's architectural splendor is a testament to the craftsmanship and artistry of Chilean and European artisans. The theater's opulent interior, adorned with intricate details and lavish ornamentation, creates an atmosphere of grandeur and enchantment. The stage, a masterpiece of engineering, seamlessly transforms into a canvas for elaborate productions, captivating audiences with its versatility and dramatic impact.

The Teatro Municipal de Santiago's programming boasts a remarkable diversity, catering to a wide range of artistic tastes and preferences. Opera enthusiasts are mesmerized by the theater's grand productions, featuring renowned singers and orchestras interpreting classic masterpieces. Classical music lovers are treated to the finest symphonic performances, showcasing the talent of world-class musicians.

Ballet performances at the Teatro Municipal de Santiago are a visual feast, with dancers gliding across the stage with grace and precision, accompanied by the enchanting melodies of renowned composers. Contemporary dance productions bring a fresh perspective to the stage, showcasing innovative choreography and captivating narratives.

Beyond its renowned performances, the Teatro Municipal de Santiago actively promotes the development of Chilean artists and fosters a love for the arts among the community. The theater's educational programs introduce young audiences to the world of opera, ballet, and classical music, nurturing their appreciation for these art forms.

The Teatro Municipal de Santiago stands as a beacon of artistic excellence in Santiago, offering a platform for world-class performances and fostering a vibrant cultural scene. The theater's rich history, architectural splendor, and diverse programming make it a must-visit destination for any traveler seeking an unforgettable cultural experience in Chile.

GRAN TEATRO NACIONAL

Chilean National Theater, formally called the Teatro Nacional Chileno (TNCH), is a performing arts venue located in Santiago, Chile. It is the country's national theater and one of the most important cultural institutions in Chile. The TNCH was inaugurated in 2005 and is located in the Centro Cultural Gabriela Mistral, a complex of cultural institutions in the heart of Santiago. The TNCH has a capacity of 1,500 seats and hosts a variety of performances, including opera, ballet, theater, and classical music.

Here is the link to the Gran Teatro Nacional's website: http://www.tnch.uchile.cl/

The Gran Teatro Nacional is located at Morandé 25, 8340648 Santiago, Región Metropolitana, Chile.

CENTRO CULTURAL GABRIELA MISTRAL

Nestled in the heart of Santiago, Chile, the Centro Cultural Gabriela Mistral, fondly known as GAM, stands as a vibrant tapestry of arts, culture, and education. This architectural marvel, named after the Nobel Prize-winning Chilean poet Gabriela Mistral, has transformed the city's cultural landscape since its inauguration in 2010.

GAM's striking design, inspired by the works of Chilean architect Gabriela Mistral, seamlessly blends modern aesthetics with a touch of traditional Chilean heritage. The complex's sprawling grounds encompass a variety of spaces, each dedicated to fostering creativity, knowledge, and artistic expression.

The heart of GAM is its Teatro Nacional Chileno, a magnificent performing arts venue that hosts a diverse array of productions, from opera and ballet to contemporary dance and theatrical performances. The theater's state-of-the-art facilities and acoustics provide an unparalleled setting for world-class performances that captivate audiences of all ages.

Beyond its theatrical offerings, GAM is a haven for art enthusiasts. The Museo Nacional de Arte Contemporáneo, housed within GAM's walls, showcases a dynamic collection of contemporary Chilean and international art, challenging perceptions and sparking new ideas. The museum's temporary exhibitions, along with its permanent collection, offer a captivating glimpse into the ever-evolving world of contemporary art.

For those seeking literary inspiration, GAM's Biblioteca Nacional de Chile, the country's national library, provides a sanctuary of knowledge and literary treasures. The library's vast collection of books, manuscripts, and historical documents spans centuries, offering a rich tapestry of Chilean and international literature.

GAM's commitment to education extends beyond its library. The complex houses a variety of classrooms, workshops, and meeting spaces that cater to diverse learning needs and interests. From art and music classes to language workshops and lectures, GAM provides a platform for lifelong learning and personal growth.

As the sun sets, GAM transforms into a vibrant hub of nightlife. The complex's cafes and restaurants come alive with lively chatter and laughter, while its open-air plazas host cultural events, concerts, and film screenings under the stars. GAM's vibrant atmosphere extends into the night, offering a unique blend of entertainment and cultural immersion.

Centro Cultural Gabriela Mistral is more than just a cultural center; it is a living embodiment of Chile's artistic spirit and cultural diversity. It is a place where creativity flourishes, knowledge is shared, and the arts come alive. Whether you're seeking theatrical thrills, artistic inspiration, or simply a place to relax and soak up the vibrant atmosphere, GAM is an essential destination in Santiago's cultural landscape.

Here are some of the things you can do at Centro Cultural Gabriela Mistral:

- Attend a performance at the Teatro Nacional Chileno.

- Explore the exhibitions at the Museo Nacional de Arte Contemporáneo.

- Browse the vast collection of books at the Biblioteca Nacional de Chile.

- Take an art or music class.

- Attend a lecture or workshop.

- Enjoy a meal at one of the cafes or restaurants.

- Relax in one of the open-air plazas.

- Attend a concert or film screening.

Centro Cultural Gabriela Mistral is open from 9:00 AM to 10:00 PM Monday through Sunday.

Here is how to get to Centro Cultural Gabriela Mistral:

- Metro: Take the Universidad de Chile station on Line 1 or the Cal y Canto station on Line 3.

- Bus: Take the Transantiago bus routes 1, 2, 5, 6, 11, 15, 21, 28, 40, 41, 42, 48, 54, 64, or 65.

- Car: Parking is available on-site for a fee.

Centro Cultural Gabriela Mistral is a must-visit destination for anyone interested in experiencing the rich cultural tapestry of Chile.

NIGHTLIFE

BELLAVISTA: A VIBRANT HUB OF NIGHTLIFE

Nestled within the heart of Santiago, Chile, Bellavista stands as a captivating blend of bohemia, cultural diversity, and lively nightlife. This vibrant neighborhood, renowned for its charming cobblestone streets, vibrant murals, and eclectic mix of cafes and bars, has long been a haven for artists, musicians, and free-spirited individuals.

As the sun sets, Bellavista transforms into a pulsating nightlife hub, its streets buzzing with energy and its bars and clubs echoing with the sounds of live music. From traditional Chilean folk music to contemporary electronic beats, the neighborhood's diverse musical scene caters to a wide range of tastes and preferences.

Bellavista's bars and clubs offer a variety of atmospheres, from intimate and cozy venues to spacious and energetic dance floors. Whether you're seeking a laid-back ambiance for conversation and drinks or an energetic setting for dancing the night away, Bellavista has something to offer everyone.

In addition to its bars and clubs, Bellavista hosts a variety of cultural events throughout the year, from open-air concerts and theater performances to literary readings and art exhibitions. These events further enhance the neighborhood's vibrant atmosphere, attracting a diverse crowd of locals and tourists alike.

Bellavista is more than just a nightlife destination; it is a symbol of Santiago's cultural vibrancy and artistic spirit. The neighborhood's bohemian charm, diverse musical scene, and constant buzz of activity make it a must-visit destination for anyone seeking an unforgettable nightlife experience in Chile.

Here are some of the best places to go for nightlife in Bellavista:

- **La Batuta:** This popular bar is known for its live music, which ranges from traditional Chilean folk to rock and pop.

- **La Casa en el Aire:** This rooftop bar offers stunning views of Santiago's skyline and a lively atmosphere.

- **Café Bellavista:** This classic café is a great place to relax and enjoy a traditional Chilean coffee or tea.

- **La Piojera:** This bar is famous for its cheap drinks and its lively atmosphere.

- **El Hoyo:** This bar is known for its deep-fried food and its late-night hours.

Bellavista is a great place to experience the vibrant nightlife of Santiago.

If you are looking for a romantic dinner, you might prefer to travel to a different neighborhood, but if you are looking for a fun and lively night out, Bellavista is the place to be!

PROVIDENCIA: A HAVEN OF UPSCALE ENTERTAINMENT

In the heart of Santiago, Chile, lies Providencia, a trendy district pulsating with vibrant energy and a captivating blend of upscale bars, restaurants, and nightlife options. This cosmopolitan hub, adorned with sleek skyscrapers and bustling streets, has emerged as a magnet for locals and visitors seeking a taste of Santiago's sophisticated nightlife scene.

As dusk settles, Providencia transforms into a dazzling spectacle of illuminated streets and lively establishments that cater to diverse tastes and preferences. From upscale cocktail bars and sophisticated wine bars to lively dance clubs and intimate jazz lounges, Providencia offers an eclectic mix of nightlife experiences to tantalize every palate.

For those seeking a sophisticated ambiance, Providencia's upscale cocktail bars and wine bars provide an elegant escape. Expert mixologists conjure up innovative cocktails, while knowledgeable sommeliers guide patrons through a curated selection of Chilean and international wines. The sleek interiors, attentive service, and refined atmosphere create an unforgettable experience for those seeking a touch of luxury in their nightlife adventures.

For those seeking a more energetic atmosphere, Providencia's lively dance clubs and vibrant music venues offer an electrifying escape. The pulsating rhythms of electronic dance music, the infectious beats of salsa, and the soulful melodies of live bands fill the air, inviting patrons to move to the rhythm and let loose. The energetic dance floors, vibrant lighting, and enthusiastic crowds create an unforgettable atmosphere for those seeking to dance the night away.

Beyond its bars and clubs, Providencia also boasts a thriving culinary scene, offering a diverse array of restaurants that cater to every taste bud. From Michelin-starred establishments to casual eateries, Providencia's dining scene provides a culinary adventure that complements the district's vibrant nightlife.

Providencia's nightlife scene is not just about the bars and clubs; it's about the ambiance, the energy, and the people. It's a place where you can dress up or dress down, where you can let loose and have fun, or where you can simply relax and enjoy the company of others. Whether you're a local or a visitor, Providencia's nightlife scene is sure to leave you with an unforgettable experience.

Here are some of the best places to go for nightlife in Providencia:

- **The Clinic:** This upscale cocktail bar is known for its innovative cocktails and sophisticated atmosphere.

- **Winebar by Vinoteca:** This wine bar is a great place to try a variety of Chilean and international wines.

- **Club Subterraneo:** This live music venue hosts a variety of bands, from local indie rock to international acts.

- **Mambo Jambo:** This salsa club is a great place to learn how to dance salsa or simply enjoy the lively atmosphere.

- **Jazz Corner:** This jazz lounge is a great place to relax and enjoy some smooth jazz music.

Providencia is a must-visit destination for anyone seeking an upscale and sophisticated nightlife experience in Santiago. With its diverse array of bars, clubs, and restaurants, Providencia offers something to everyone, from those seeking a touch of elegance to those seeking an energetic escape. So, come and experience the vibrant nightlife of Providencia and let yourself be swept away by the rhythm of the city.

LASTARRIA: A BOHEMIAN OASIS IN SANTIAGO'S HEART

In the heart of Santiago, Chile, nestled amidst the city's vibrant pulse, lies the charming neighborhood of Lastarria, an oasis of bohemian spirit, artistic expression, and captivating history. Once the home of Chile's elite, Lastarria has transformed into a haven for artists, musicians, and free-thinkers, its cobblestone streets echoing with creativity and a touch of eccentricity.

Strolling through Lastarria's labyrinthine lanes, you'll be captivated by its architectural charm, a harmonious blend of 19th-century buildings and contemporary structures. Majestic mansions with ornate facades stand alongside modern art galleries, their contrasting styles creating a captivating visual tapestry. The neighborhood's plazas and courtyards offer tranquil respites, adorned with lush greenery and inviting fountains, providing a welcome escape from the city's bustling energy.

As the sun begins to set, Lastarria transforms into a bohemian wonderland, its streets illuminated by the warm glow of cafes and bars. The air fills with the enticing aroma of freshly brewed coffee and tantalizing dishes, drawing in locals and visitors alike. Cozy cafes tucked away in charming corners offer a perfect setting for leisurely conversations and indulging in the neighborhood's delightful culinary creations.

Lastarria's nightlife is an electrifying blend of traditional Chilean music, lively salsa beats, and contemporary electronic sounds. Music venues, ranging from intimate cafes to open-air plazas, showcase the neighborhood's vibrant musical scene, providing a stage for local talent and international acts alike. As the night progresses, Lastarria's streets come alive with the rhythm of music and the energy of free expression.

Lastarria is a neighborhood that caters to all tastes. For those seeking a touch of sophistication, Lastarria's upscale bars and cocktail lounges offer an elegant escape, while the neighborhood's dive bars and pubs provide a more laid-back atmosphere for mingling with locals and enjoying casual conversations.

Beyond its bars and cafes, Lastarria is also home to a thriving cultural scene. Numerous art galleries showcase the works of local and international artists, while theater performances and literary readings add to the neighborhood's vibrant cultural tapestry. Lastarria's commitment to the arts extends beyond its galleries and theaters; the neighborhood's walls are adorned with vibrant murals that depict scenes from Chilean history, folklore, and contemporary art, transforming the streets into an open-air art gallery.

Lastarria is more than just a neighborhood; it's a living embodiment of Santiago's bohemian spirit and artistic soul. It's a place where creativity thrives, where individuality is celebrated, and where the city's history and culture intertwine with a touch of eccentricity. Whether you're seeking artistic inspiration, a taste of Santiago's vibrant nightlife, or simply a place to wander and immerse yourself in the city's captivating charm, Lastarria is an essential part of Santiago's vibrant tapestry.

CHAPTER 4: CULINARY DELIGHTS

Santiago, Chile, is a vibrant city with a rich culinary scene, offering a diverse array of flavors and dining experiences to tantalize every palate. From traditional Chilean fare to international cuisine, Santiago's restaurants cater to a wide range of tastes and preferences, ensuring that every visitor can find something to satisfy their cravings.

Traditional Chilean Cuisine

No culinary adventure in Santiago is complete without sampling the city's traditional dishes, which showcase the country's rich agricultural heritage and unique culinary traditions. Here are some of the must-try Chilean dishes:

- **Empanadas:** These savory pastries are filled with a variety of fillings, from ground beef and onions to seafood and cheese. Empanadas are a popular snack, often served with aji, a spicy chili sauce.

Empanadas, Chilean food

- Pastel de choclo: This creamy corn pie is a classic Chilean dish, typically served with a side salad or rice.

Pastel de choclo, Chilean food

- **Curanto:** This hearty stew is a specialty of Chiloé Island, located in southern Chile. Curanto is made with a variety of meats, seafood, and vegetables, and is traditionally cooked underground in a hot stone oven.

Curanto, Chilean food

- **Pichanga:** This mixed platter is a Chilean favorite, featuring a variety of fried meats, cheeses, and vegetables. Pichanga is often served as a shared dish and is perfect for a casual gathering.

Pichanga, Chilean food

International Cuisine

Santiago also boasts a thriving international culinary scene, with restaurants serving cuisine from all corners of the globe. From Italian trattorias to Japanese sushi bars, Santiago's diverse dining options ensure that there is something to satisfy every craving.

For those seeking a taste of Italy, Santiago offers a variety of authentic Italian restaurants, serving wood-fired pizzas, fresh pasta dishes, and delectable tiramisu. For a taste of Japan, Santiago's sushi bars offer a wide variety of sushi rolls, sashimi platters, and tempura dishes.

In addition to Italian and Japanese cuisine, Santiago also offers restaurants serving cuisine from India, Thailand, Mexico, and other countries. This diversity of international restaurants reflects Santiago's cosmopolitan status and its growing global influence.

Dining Experiences

Santiago offers a variety of dining experiences to suit all tastes and budgets. From casual cafes and street food vendors to upscale fine-dining establishments, Santiago's restaurants provide an array of settings to enjoy the city's culinary delights.

For a casual and authentic Chilean dining experience, consider visiting one of the city's many neighborhood cafes or parrillas, which are grill restaurants specializing in meat dishes. For a more upscale dining experience, Santiago offers a variety of fine-dining restaurants, many of which are located in the trendy neighborhoods of Providencia and Las Condes.

No matter what your budget or preferences, Santiago's culinary scene has something to offer everyone. So, come and embark on a gastronomic adventure through the streets of Santiago and discover the city's rich and diverse culinary offerings.

EMPANADAS: A PASTRY FILLED WITH MEAT, CHEESE, OR VEGETABLES

Empanadas are a staple of Chilean cuisine, enjoyed by locals and visitors alike. These savory pastries are filled with a variety of delicious fillings, from hearty ground beef and onions to succulent seafood and tangy cheese. Empanadas are a popular snack or light meal, often served with aji, a spicy chili sauce that adds a zesty kick to the flavors.

TYPES OF EMPANADAS;

Chilean empanadas come in a variety of shapes and sizes, but they all share one common characteristic: their flaky, golden crust. The fillings, however, vary widely, reflecting the diverse culinary influences in Chile. Here are some of the most popular empanada fillings:

Empanadas de pino, Chilean food

- **Empanadas de pino:** This classic empanada is filled with ground beef, onions, raisins, olives, and a hard-boiled egg.

- **Empanadas de mariscos:** These seafood empanadas are filled with a mixture of shrimp, crab, and other shellfish, often seasoned with lemon juice and cilantro.

- Empanadas de queso: Cheese empanadas are a simple yet

satisfying option, filled with a creamy blend of cheese, often with a hint of spice or herbs.

Empanadas de queso, Chilean food

- Empanadas de verduras: Vegetarian empanadas are filled with a variety of vegetables, such as spinach, carrots, and corn.

WHERE TO FIND EMPANADAS

Empanadas are ubiquitous in Chile, and they can be found everywhere from street vendors and casual cafes to upscale restaurants. Some of the best empanadas in Santiago can be found in the following neighborhoods:

- La Piojera: This legendary restaurant in Bellavista is famous for its cheap and delicious empanadas.

La Piojera, Santiago, Chile

- El Nacional: This historic restaurant in Barrio Brasil offers a wide variety of empanadas, including traditional and innovative fillings.

El Nacional, Santiago, Chile

- Empanadas de María Luisa: This popular chain has locations throughout Santiago and is known for its consistent quality and delicious empanadas.

Empanadas de María Luisa, Santiago, Chile

EMPANADAS: A CULINARY DELIGHT

Empanadas are more than just a snack; they are a symbol of Chilean culture and cuisine. These savory pastries perfectly encapsulate the country's rich culinary heritage and its love for fresh, flavorful ingredients. So, come and experience the culinary delight of Chilean empanadas and discover the diverse flavors that have made them a beloved dish around the world.

PASTEL DE CHOCLO

Pastel de choclo, a traditional Chilean corn casserole, is a culinary delight that has captivated taste buds for generations. This savory dish, typically served during the winter months, is a comforting blend of creamy corn, tender meat, and a hint of sweetness. The casserole's rich flavors and hearty ingredients make it a staple in Chilean households, often served as a main course or a side dish.

The Essence of Pastel de Choclo

At the heart of pastel de choclo lies a creamy corn mixture, prepared by simmering fresh corn kernels with milk, butter, and a touch of sugar. This corn base is then enriched with a flavorful meat mixture, traditionally made with ground beef, onions, garlic, and spices. The casserole's layers are then topped with a layer of sliced hard-boiled eggs and a sprinkle of sugar, adding a touch of sweetness and visual appeal.

Variations and Culinary Delights

While the classic pastel de choclo recipe remains a culinary mainstay, there are regional variations that add a unique twist to this beloved dish. In some regions, raisins or olives are added to the meat mixture, while others incorporate chicken or pork instead of beef. The casserole's versatility extends to its toppings, with some cooks opting for a sprinkle of grated Parmesan cheese or a dollop of sour cream.

Serving Pastel de Choclo

Pastel de choclo is typically served hot from the oven, its golden crust glistening with melted cheese. The casserole is often accompanied by a side salad or a simple rice dish, providing a refreshing contrast to the rich flavors of the corn mixture and meat.

A Culinary Icon

Pastel de choclo transcends its culinary role, serving as a symbol of Chilean culture and heritage. The dish's presence at family gatherings and special occasions signifies warmth, comfort, and the enduring traditions of Chilean cuisine.

So, if you're seeking a culinary adventure that captures the essence of Chile, come and savor the delicious pastel de choclo. Indulge in its creamy corn mixture, succulent meat, and a touch of sweetness, and discover why this traditional casserole has remained a beloved dish for generations.

ASADO: A BARBEQUE

Asado is more than just a barbeque; it is a social event that brings people together. Asado is a way for friends and family to gather, enjoy good food, and celebrate life. Asado is also a way to showcase Chilean culture and traditions, as it is a dish that has been enjoyed for generations.

The Asado Process

Asado is typically prepared over an open fire or grill, using wood or charcoal. The meat is cooked slowly over a low heat, allowing it to develop a rich, smoky flavor. Asado is typically made with beef, but it can also be made with pork, chicken, or lamb.

The Asado Menu

Asado is typically served with a variety of side dishes, such as grilled vegetables, potatoes, and salads. Asado is also often accompanied by a variety of alcoholic beverages, such as wine, beer, or pisco sours.

Asado in Chile

Asado is a popular dish throughout Chile, but it is especially popular in the southern regions of the country, where there is a strong tradition of grilling meat. Asado is often served at family gatherings, special occasions, and even everyday meals.

Asado: A Culinary Icon

Asado is a culinary icon that represents Chilean culture and heritage. Asado is a dish that is enjoyed by people of all ages and backgrounds, and it is a reminder of the importance of food and community in Chilean life.

Here are some tips for hosting an asado:

- Choose the right meat. The best cuts of meat for asado are those that are well-marbled, such as ribeye, New York strip, or flank steak.

- Marinate the meat. Marinating the meat will help to tenderize it and add flavor.

- Cook the meat slowly over a low heat. This will help to

develop the rich, smoky flavor that is characteristic of asado.

- Serve the asado with a variety of side dishes. This will help to balance out the richness of the meat.

Enjoy your asado!

CURANTO: A TRADITIONAL STEW

Curanto, a traditional stew from Chiloé Island in southern Chile, is a culinary masterpiece that showcases the region's rich agricultural heritage and unique culinary traditions. This hearty and flavorful dish is a testament to the ingenuity of Chiloé's inhabitants, who have adapted their cooking methods to the island's unique climate and resources.

A Dish Rooted in Tradition

Curanto's origins can be traced back to the indigenous Mapuche people, who inhabited Chiloé Island for centuries. The Mapuche traditionally cooked curanto in underground ovens, using hot stones to heat the food. This method of cooking, known as curanto en hoyo, is still used today by some Chiloé families, and it is considered to be the most authentic way to prepare the dish.

A Culinary Symphony of Flavors

Curanto is a true symphony of flavors, featuring a variety of meats, seafood, vegetables, and potatoes. The traditional ingredients include beef, pork, chicken, shellfish, potatoes, nalca (a type of Chilean rhubarb), and chapaleles (potato dumplings). These ingredients are layered in a large pot or underground oven and cooked over hot stones until they are tender and infused with a rich and smoky flavor.

A Culinary Adventure

Enjoying curanto is a culinary adventure in itself. The dish is typically served on a large communal platter, and diners use wooden spoons to scoop up the various ingredients. The combination of flavors and textures is truly unique, and curanto is sure to tantalize the taste buds of even the most discerning palate.

Curanto: A Symbol of Chiloé's Culture

Curanto is more than just a dish; it is a symbol of Chiloé's culture and its deep connection to the land and sea. The dish is often served at special occasions, such as weddings, festivals, and family gatherings. Curanto is also a reminder of the resilience and resourcefulness of the Chiloé people, who have adapted their culinary traditions to the island's unique environment.

So, if you're ever in southern Chile, be sure to seek out a curanto and experience this culinary masterpiece for yourself.

Here are some tips for enjoying curanto:

- Be patient. Curanto can take several hours to cook, so be prepared to wait.

- Come hungry. Curanto is a hearty dish, so come with a big appetite.

- Be adventurous. Don't be afraid to try new things. Curanto is a dish that is full of surprises.

- Enjoy the company. Curanto is best enjoyed with friends and family.

Buen provecho!

CHORRILLANA: A FRIED SEAFOOD DISH

Chorrillana, a traditional Peruvian seafood dish, is a culinary delight that has captivated taste buds for generations. This vibrant and savory dish, originating from the coastal town of Chorrillos in Lima, Peru, has become an emblem of the country's rich culinary heritage and its love for fresh, flavorful seafood.

A Culinary Mosaic

Chorrillana is a feast for the eyes as much as it is for the palate. The dish is a colorful tapestry of fried seafood, typically including fish, shrimp, calamari, and mussels, nestled atop a bed of golden French fries. This harmonious blend of textures and flavors is further enhanced by a drizzle of a tangy and spicy sauce, often prepared with tomatoes, onions, garlic, and aji amarillo, a Peruvian chili pepper.

The Essence of Chorrillana

At the heart of Chorrillana lies the freshest seafood, carefully selected and expertly prepared. The fish, typically a white-fleshed variety like corvina or sole, is delicately battered and fried to golden perfection, preserving its tender texture and delicate flavor. Shrimp, calamari, and mussels are also cooked to perfection, ensuring their succulent texture and briny sweetness.

A Culinary Symphony of Flavors

The golden French fries provide a delightful contrast to the crispy seafood, their starchy goodness complementing the seafood's savory flavors. The tangy and spicy sauce, often infused with the vibrant aroma of aji amarillo, adds a zesty kick to the dish, awakening the taste buds with its fiery touch.

Serving Chorrillana

Chorrillana is typically served as a main course, its generous portions satisfying even the most ravenous appetites. The dish is often accompanied by a side of rice or a simple salad, providing a refreshing contrast to its rich flavors.

Chorrillana: A Culinary Legacy

Chorrillana transcends its culinary role, serving as a symbol of Peruvian culture and heritage. The dish's presence at family gatherings, special occasions, and even everyday meals signifies warmth, comfort, and the enduring traditions of Peruvian cuisine.

So, if you're seeking a culinary adventure that captures the essence of Peru, come and savor the delightful Chorrillana. Indulge in its crispy seafood, golden French fries, and tangy sauce, and discover why this traditional dish has remained a beloved culinary icon for generations.

CHILEAN WINE

CONCHA Y TORO

Concha y Toro, the largest producer and exporter of wines from Latin America, is a Chilean winery with a rich history and a global reputation for producing high-quality wines. With over 10,000 hectares of vineyards under cultivation in Chile, Argentina, and the United States, Concha y Toro produces a wide range of wines, from entry-level to premium, that cater to a diverse range of palates.

A Legacy of Excellence

Concha y Toro's roots can be traced back to 1855 when Melchor Concha y Toro, a prominent Chilean politician and businessman, established the winery in Pirque Valley, just outside of Santiago. Concha y Toro's early success was driven by its commitment to quality and innovation, and the winery quickly gained recognition for its superior wines.

A Global Winemaking Leader

Today, Concha y Toro is one of the most respected names in the world of wine. The winery's wines are exported to over 135 countries, and they have consistently received high scores from wine critics around the globe. Concha y Toro has also been recognized for its sustainable winemaking practices, and the winery is a leader in environmental initiatives in the wine industry.

Concha y Toro's Iconic Wines

Concha y Toro produces a wide range of wines, but some of its most iconic brands include:

- Casillero del Diablo: This is Concha y Toro's most popular brand, and it is known for its approachable and affordable wines.

Casillero del Diablo, Chilean wine

- Don Melchor: This is Concha y Toro's flagship wine, and it is a Bordeaux-style blend that has been consistently rated among the best wines in Chile.

Don Melchor, Chilean wine

- Marqués de Casa Concha: This is a range of premium wines

that are made from some of Concha y Toro's best vineyards.

Marqués de Casa Concha, Chilean wine

Visiting Concha y Toro

Concha y Toro's main winery is located in Pirque Valley, and it is open to visitors for tours and tastings. The winery also has a number of other visitor centers in Chile, Argentina, and the United States.

Concha y Toro: A Chilean Wine Icon

Concha y Toro is more than just a winery; it is an icon of Chilean winemaking. The winery's commitment to quality, innovation, and sustainability has made it one of the most respected names in the world of wine. So, if you're seeking a taste of Chilean winemaking excellence, be sure to explore the wines of Concha y Toro.

VIÑA SANTA CRUZ

Located in the Colchagua Valley, Viña Santa Cruz is a Chilean winery renowned for its exceptional wines and captivating vineyard setting. Nestled amidst rolling hills and picturesque landscapes, the winery offers an idyllic retreat for wine enthusiasts and nature lovers alike.

A Legacy of Passion for Wine

Viña Santa Cruz's story began in 2003 when Carlos Cardoen, a visionary Chilean businessman with a deep appreciation for winemaking, embarked on a journey to create a winery that would embody the essence of Chile's terroir and heritage. Driven by a passion for excellence and a commitment to sustainable practices, Cardoen sought to establish Viña Santa Cruz as a beacon of Chilean winemaking excellence.

A Sanctuary of Sustainable Winemaking

Viña Santa Cruz's vineyards span 150 hectares in the Lolol region of the Colchagua Valley, a terroir renowned for its ideal conditions for grape cultivation. The winery's dedication to sustainability is evident in its meticulous viticultural practices, which emphasize minimal intervention and respect for the delicate balance of the ecosystem.

A Symphony of Flavors

Viña Santa Cruz produces a diverse range of wines, each showcasing the unique character of the Colchagua Valley's terroir. From elegant Chardonnay and Sauvignon Blanc to bold Cabernet Sauvignon and Carmenère, the winery's wines are consistently praised for their balance, complexity, and elegance.

An Enchanting Vineyard Experience

Beyond its exceptional wines, Viña Santa Cruz offers visitors an unforgettable vineyard experience. The winery's modern facilities, nestled amidst the picturesque vineyards, provide a welcoming setting for wine tastings, guided tours, and special events. Visitors can immerse themselves in the world of winemaking, learn about the intricate processes involved, and discover the passion that drives the winery's team.

A Culinary Adventure

Viña Santa Cruz's culinary offerings complement the winery's exceptional wines, creating a harmonious blend of flavors and experiences. The winery's restaurant, La Vinoteca, offers a menu of Chilean cuisine, showcasing fresh, seasonal ingredients and highlighting the flavors of the region.

A Destination for Wine Enthusiasts

Viña Santa Cruz has established itself as a premier destination for wine enthusiasts seeking an exceptional winemaking experience. The winery's commitment to quality, sustainability, and innovation has earned it numerous accolades, including the title of "Best Winery in Colchagua Valley" at the 2018 Chile Wine Awards.

A Fusion of Wine and Nature

Viña Santa Cruz is more than just a winery; it is a sanctuary where wine and nature converge. The winery's breathtaking vineyard setting, coupled with its exceptional wines and warm hospitality, creates an unforgettable experience for visitors from around the globe.

Whether you're a seasoned wine connoisseur or a curious newcomer, Viña Santa Cruz invites you to embark on a journey of discovery, where the essence of Chilean winemaking comes alive.

VIÑA MONTES

Nestled amidst the rolling hills and verdant vineyards of the Apalta Valley in Chile's Colchagua Valley, Viña Montes stands as a testament to the country's rich winemaking heritage and its unwavering pursuit of excellence. Founded in 1988 by a group of visionary winemakers, Viña Montes has revolutionized the Chilean wine industry, establishing a reputation for producing high-quality wines that have captivated palates worldwide.

A Journey of Innovation and Excellence

Viña Montes' story began with a bold vision to challenge the status quo and elevate Chilean winemaking to the global stage. The winery's founders, driven by a passion for innovation and a deep respect for Chilean terroir, embarked on a journey to create wines that would showcase the country's unique grape varieties and diverse terroirs.

From its inception, Viña Montes embraced sustainable practices that prioritize the environment and the delicate balance of the ecosystem. The winery's vineyards are meticulously managed, employing organic and biodynamic techniques to ensure the health of the vines and the preservation of the land.

A Symphony of Chilean Terroirs

Viña Montes' vineyards span over 1,000 hectares across Chile's most prestigious wine regions, including Colchagua, Aconcagua, Maipo, and Apalta. Each terroir imparts its unique character to the wines, resulting in a diverse portfolio that reflects the rich tapestry of Chilean viticulture.

The winery's flagship wine, Montes Alpha Cabernet Sauvignon, is a testament to its dedication to producing world-class wines. This iconic blend consistently earns accolades from international critics, showcasing the winery's mastery of Cabernet Sauvignon and its ability to express the true essence of Chilean terroir.

An Unforgettable Wine Experience

Viña Montes offers visitors an immersive wine experience, inviting them to discover the passion and dedication that goes into every bottle. Guided tours through the winery's state-of-the-art facilities provide insights into the winemaking process, while personalized tastings allow visitors to savor the winery's exceptional wines and appreciate their unique character.

A Legacy of Chilean Winemaking Excellence

Viña Montes has established itself as a pioneer in Chilean winemaking, paving the way for other wineries to follow its lead in producing high-quality wines that have garnered international recognition. The winery's commitment to innovation, sustainability, and the pursuit of excellence has cemented its place as a benchmark for Chilean winemaking.

A Must-Visit Destination for Wine Enthusiasts

For wine enthusiasts seeking an unforgettable wine experience, Viña Montes is an essential destination. The winery's breathtaking vineyard setting, coupled with its exceptional wines and warm hospitality, creates a journey of discovery that encapsulates the essence of Chilean winemaking.

COUSIÑO MACUL

Nestled amidst the picturesque landscapes of the Maipo Valley, Cousiño Macul stands as a beacon of Chilean winemaking heritage, boasting a lineage that stretches back to 1856. Founded by Matias Cousiño, a visionary entrepreneur with a deep passion for wine, Cousiño Macul has consistently produced exceptional wines that embody the essence of Chilean terroir and reflect the winery's unwavering commitment to quality and tradition.

A Legacy of Excellence

From its inception, Cousiño Macul has been guided by a profound respect for the land and a dedication to sustainable winemaking practices. The winery's vineyards, spanning over 1,300 hectares in the

Maipo Valley, are meticulously managed, employing organic and biodynamic techniques to ensure the health of the vines and the preservation of the ecosystem.

Cousiño Macul's winemaking philosophy is deeply rooted in tradition, yet it embraces innovation to continuously elevate its wines to new heights. The winery's team of experienced winemakers, led by Pascal Marty, meticulously crafts each wine, balancing modern techniques with time-honored practices to showcase the unique character of the Maipo Valley's terroir.

A Symphony of Chilean Flavors

Cousiño Macul's portfolio of wines encompasses a diverse range of styles, each reflecting the winery's mastery of various grape varieties and its ability to express the nuances of the Maipo Valley's terroir. From elegant Chardonnay and Sauvignon Blanc to bold Cabernet Sauvignon and Carmenère, Cousiño Macul's wines consistently earn accolades from international critics, captivating palates worldwide.

One of Cousiño Macul's most iconic wines is the Antiguas Reservas Cabernet Sauvignon, a limited-edition wine that embodies the winery's dedication to excellence. This exceptional wine is sourced from the winery's oldest and most prized Cabernet Sauvignon vines, aged for 18 months in French oak barrels, and showcases the true depth and complexity of the Maipo Valley's terroir.

An Immersive Wine Experience

Cousiño Macul invites visitors to embark on an immersive wine experience, offering a glimpse into the world-class winemaking that takes place within its historic estate. Guided tours through the winery's picturesque vineyards and state-of-the-art facilities provide insights into the winemaking process, while personalized tastings allow visitors to savor the winery's exceptional wines and appreciate their unique character.

A Culinary Destination

Cousiño Macul's culinary offerings complement its exceptional wines, creating a harmonious blend of flavors and experiences. The winery's restaurant, Guayacán, offers a menu of Chilean cuisine, showcasing fresh, seasonal ingredients and highlighting the flavors of the region.

Cousiño Macul: A Testament to Chilean Winemaking Excellence

Cousiño Macul stands as a testament to Chile's rich winemaking heritage and its unwavering pursuit of excellence. The winery's commitment to quality, tradition, and innovation has earned it a place among the world's most respected wine producers. Whether you're a seasoned wine connoisseur or a curious newcomer, Cousiño Macul invites you to embark on a journey of discovery, where the essence of Chilean winemaking comes alive.

VIÑA ERRÁZURIZ

Nestled amidst the rolling hills and verdant vineyards of Chile's Aconcagua Valley, Viña Errázuriz stands as a beacon of Chilean winemaking excellence, renowned for its exceptional wines and unwavering commitment to sustainable practices. Founded in 1855 by Don José Errázuriz Ovalle, a visionary statesman and entrepreneur, Viña Errázuriz has established itself as a pioneer in sustainable winemaking, paving the way for a more environmentally conscious approach to viticulture and wine production.

A Legacy of Environmental Stewardship

From its inception, Viña Errázuriz has been guided by a deep respect for the land and a dedication to protecting the delicate balance of the ecosystem. The winery's vineyards, spanning over 2,500 hectares in the Aconcagua Valley, are meticulously managed, employing organic and biodynamic techniques to ensure the health of the vines, conserve water resources, and promote biodiversity.

Viña Errázuriz's commitment to sustainability extends beyond its vineyards to encompass every aspect of its operations. The winery has implemented energy-efficient practices, reduced its carbon footprint, and minimized waste generation, earning it recognition as a leader in sustainable winemaking practices.

A Symphony of Chilean Terroirs

Viña Errázuriz's vineyards span diverse microclimates within the Aconcagua Valley, each imparting its unique character to the wines. From the cool coastal influences of Aconcagua Costa to the warmer, sun-drenched slopes of Aconcagua Andes, the winery's grapes express a range of flavors and aromas that showcase the valley's exceptional terroir.

The winery's flagship wine, Don Maximiano Founder's Reserve Cabernet Sauvignon, is a testament to its dedication to producing world-class wines that reflect the essence of Chilean terroir. This iconic blend consistently earns accolades from international critics, captivating palates worldwide with its balance, complexity, and elegance.

An Unforgettable Wine Experience

Viña Errázuriz offers visitors an immersive wine experience, inviting them to discover the passion and dedication that goes into every bottle. Guided tours through the winery's historic estate and state-of-the-art facilities provide insights into the winemaking process, while personalized tastings allow visitors to savor the winery's exceptional wines and appreciate their unique character.

A Culinary Destination

Viña Errázuriz's culinary offerings complement its exceptional wines, creating a harmonious blend of flavors and experiences. The winery's restaurant, Viñedo de Errázuriz, offers a menu of Chilean cuisine, showcasing fresh, seasonal ingredients and highlighting the flavors of the region.

Viña Errázuriz: A Benchmark for Sustainable Winemaking

Viña Errázuriz stands as a benchmark for sustainable winemaking, demonstrating that exceptional wines can be produced in harmony with the environment. The winery's unwavering commitment to sustainability has earned it numerous accolades, including the title of "Sustainable Winery of the Year" at the 2021 International Wine & Spirit Competition.

A Must-Visit Destination for Wine Enthusiasts

For wine enthusiasts seeking an unforgettable wine experience while supporting sustainable practices, Viña Errázuriz is an essential destination. The winery's breathtaking vineyard setting, coupled with its exceptional wines, warm hospitality, and commitment to sustainability, creates a journey of discovery that encapsulates the essence of Chilean winemaking at its finest.

CHAPTER 5: DAY TRIPS AND EXCURSIONS

Santiago, Chile, offers a wealth of exciting day trips and excursions that allow visitors to explore the city's surroundings and delve into the country's rich culture and natural beauty. From venturing into the Andes Mountains to discovering charming coastal towns, these excursions provide a glimpse into the diverse landscapes and captivating experiences that await beyond the city limits.

ESCAPE TO THE ANDES MOUNTAINS

- **Cajón del Maipo**: Embark on a day trip to Cajón del Maipo, a picturesque natural area nestled in the foothills of the Andes Mountains. Hike through lush forests, trek along cascading waterfalls, and immerse yourself in the tranquility of nature.

Cajón del Maipo, Chile

- **Valle Nevado:** For those seeking winter sports adventures, Valle Nevado offers world-class skiing and snowboarding facilities amidst breathtaking mountain scenery.

Valle Nevado, Chile

- **Portillo:** Experience the grandeur of the Andes at

Portillo, a renowned ski resort known for its stunning lake and panoramic views.

Portillo, Chile

DISCOVER COASTAL CHARM

- **Valparaíso:** Embark on a day trip to Valparaíso, a vibrant coastal city renowned for its colorful architecture, bohemian flair, and UNESCO World Heritage status.

Valparaíso, Chile

- **Viña del Mar:** Explore the elegance of Viña del Mar, a seaside resort town known for its beautiful beaches, manicured parks, and luxurious casinos.

Viña del Mar, Chile

- **Isla Negra:** Immerse yourself in the life and works of Nobel laureate Pablo Neruda by visiting his iconic residence, Isla Negra, located in the coastal town of Isla Negra.

Isla Negra, Chile

EXPLORE CULTURAL GEMS

- **Colchagua Valley:** Embark on a wine-tasting adventure in the Colchagua Valley, renowned for its exceptional wines and picturesque vineyards.

Colchagua Valley, Chile

- **Aconcagua Valley:** Discover the Aconcagua Valley, home to the world's highest mountain,

Cerro Aconcagua, and a thriving wine industry.

Aconcagua Valley, Chile

- **Maipo Valley:** Explore the Maipo Valley, the cradle of Chilean winemaking, and indulge in wine tastings amidst stunning scenery.

Maipo Valley, Chile

These day trips and excursions offer just a glimpse into the diverse experiences that await beyond

Santiago. Whether seeking adventure in the mountains, exploring coastal towns, or immersing yourself in Chilean culture, these excursions provide a taste of the country's rich heritage and natural beauty.

VALPARAÍSO

Nestled along Chile's Pacific coastline, Valparaíso is a captivating city that bursts with color, culture, and history. Renowned for its UNESCO World Heritage-listed historic quarter, Valparaíso is a labyrinth of winding streets, hillside ascensors, and eclectic architecture that paints a vibrant portrait of Chilean heritage. As you explore the city's maze-like alleys, you'll discover hidden plazas, charming cafés, and lively street art that showcase the city's artistic soul.

EXPLORING VALPARAÍSO'S ENCHANTING CHARM

1. **Cerro Alegre and Cerro Concepción:** Ascend to the hilltops of Cerro Alegre and Cerro Concepción, two of Valparaíso's most iconic neighborhoods. Admire the colorful houses adorned with murals and intricate street art, and soak in the panoramic views of the city and harbor.

Cerro Alegre and Cerro Concepción, Valparaíso, Chile

2. **Plaza Sotomayor:** Visit Plaza Sotomayor, the heart of Valparaíso's historic quarter. Pay homage to the naval heroes who fought in the Battle of Iquique, and admire the imposing monument that stands as a testament to their bravery.

Plaza Sotomayor, Valparaíso, Chile

3. **Paseo Yugoslavo:** Stroll along Paseo Yugoslavo, a picturesque promenade that offers breathtaking views of the bay. As you walk, admire the majestic Palacio Baburizza, a striking architectural landmark that now houses the Municipal Museum of Fine Arts.

Paseo Yugoslavo, Valparaíso, Chile

4. **La Sebastiana:** Embark on a journey to La Sebastiana, the former residence of Chilean poet Pablo Neruda. Discover the eccentric beauty of this whimsical house-turned-museum, filled with Neruda's personal collections and offering stunning views of the city.

La Sebastiana, Valparaíso, Chile

5. **Ascensores de Valparaíso:** Experience the thrill of riding Valparaíso's iconic funiculars, or ascensores, which connect the city's lower and upper

districts. Enjoy the panoramic views as you ascend the hills, and appreciate the ingenuity of these historic transportation systems.

Ascensores de Valparaíso, Chile

6. **Muelle Barón:** Wander along Muelle Barón, a lively pier that buzzes with activity. Sample fresh seafood at local restaurants, browse souvenir stands, and watch street performers entertain the crowds.

Muelle Barón, Valparaíso, Chile

7. **Playa Cavancha:** Escape to Playa Cavancha, a popular beach with a relaxed atmosphere. Sunbathe on the golden sands, take a refreshing dip in the Pacific Ocean, or enjoy a leisurely stroll along the seaside promenade.

Playa Cavancha, Valparaíso, Chile

8. **Mercado El Cardonal:** Immerse yourself in the vibrant atmosphere of Mercado El Cardonal, a bustling marketplace where fresh produce, local crafts, and enticing aromas fill the air. Sample traditional Chilean cuisine, savor fresh seafood, and discover unique souvenirs.

Mercado El Cardonal, Valparaíso, Chile

9. **Pasaje Esmeralda:** Explore Pasaje Esmeralda, a narrow alleyway transformed into an open-air art gallery. Admire the colorful murals that adorn the walls, capturing the essence of Valparaíso's vibrant spirit.

Pasaje Esmeralda, Valparaíso, Chile

10. **Parque Cultural Cerro Cárcel:** Visit Parque Cultural Cerro Cárcel, a former prison transformed into a cultural hub. Explore art exhibitions, attend theater performances, and enjoy panoramic views of the city from the hilltop park.

Parque Cultural Cerro Cárcel, Valparaíso, Chile

Valparaíso is a city that captures the heart and ignites the senses. With its captivating blend of history, culture, and natural beauty, Valparaíso offers an unforgettable experience for every traveler.

VIÑA DEL MAR

Nestled along Chile's Pacific coast, Viña del Mar is a sophisticated seaside resort town known for its beautiful beaches, manicured parks, and luxurious casinos. The city is a popular destination for both Chileans and foreign tourists, who flock to its shores to enjoy the sun, sand, and sea.

EXPLORING VIÑA DEL MAR'S CHARM

1. **Playa Caleta Abarca:** Relax on the golden sands of Playa Caleta Abarca, one of Viña del Mar's most popular beaches.

Take a refreshing dip in the Pacific Ocean, or sunbathe under the Chilean sun.

Playa Caleta Abarca, Viña del Mar, Chile

2. **Parque Quinta Vergara:** Visit Parque Quinta Vergara, a sprawling park that offers stunning views of the city and ocean. Stroll through the gardens, visit the orchidarium, or catch a concert or show at the Quinta Vergara Amphitheater.

Parque Quinta Vergara, Viña del Mar, Chile

3. **Casino Municipal de Viña del Mar:** Try your luck at the Casino Municipal de Viña del Mar, one of the largest casinos in South America. Enjoy a night of gambling, fine dining, and entertainment.

Casino Municipal de Viña del Mar, Viña del Mar, Chile

4. **Palacio Vergara:** Explore Palacio Vergara, a stunning Italianate-style mansion that now houses the Museum of Fine Arts of Viña del Mar. Admire the collection of Chilean and international art, or simply enjoy the beauty of the gardens.

Palacio Vergara, Viña del Mar, Chile

5. **Balneario Municipal de Viña del Mar:** Take a stroll along Balneario Municipal de Viña del Mar, a popular promenade that offers stunning views of the ocean. Enjoy the fresh air, people-watch, or simply relax and soak up the sun.

6. **Playa de los Enamorados:** Escape to Playa de los Enamorados, a secluded beach perfect for a romantic getaway. Bask in the sun, swim in the ocean, or simply enjoy each other's company.

Playa de los Enamorados, Viña del Mar, Chile

7. **Museo Fonck:** Visit Museo Fonck, a museum that houses a collection of Chilean and international art, including sculptures, paintings, and archaeological artifacts.

Museo Fonck, Viña del Mar, Chile

8. **Quinta de los Reyes:** Visit Quinta de los Reyes, a former summer home of the Chilean royal family. Explore the gardens, visit the museum, or simply enjoy the tranquility of the setting.

Quinta de los Reyes, Viña del Mar, Chile

9. **Reloj de Flores:** Admire the Reloj de Flores, a flower clock

that is one of Viña del Mar's most iconic landmarks. The clock is decorated with colorful flowers that change with the seasons.

Reloj de Flores, Viña del Mar, Chile

10. **Festival Internacional de la Canción de Viña del Mar:** Attend the Festival Internacional de la Canción de Viña del Mar, a popular music festival that takes place every February. The festival features performances by international and Chilean artists, and is a major cultural event in Chile.

Festival Internacional de la Canción de Viña del Mar, Viña del Mar, Chile

Viña del Mar is a city that offers something for everyone. Whether you're looking to relax on the beach, explore the city's cultural attractions, or simply enjoy the Chilean sun, Viña del Mar is the perfect destination for your next vacation.

CAJÓN DEL MAIPO

Nestled amidst the foothills of the towering Andes Mountains, Cajón del Maipo is a captivating mountain resort area just outside Santiago, Chile. Renowned for its breathtaking natural beauty, Cajón del Maipo offers an abundance of outdoor activities, from invigorating hikes and exhilarating mountain biking trails to thrilling white-water rafting adventures.

EMBARK ON SCENIC HIKES

1. **Embalse El Yeso:** Lace up your hiking boots and embark on a scenic trek to Embalse El Yeso, a stunning turquoise reservoir surrounded by snow-capped peaks. Capture breathtaking views of the reservoir and its reflection of the Andes Mountains.

Embalse El Yeso, Cajón del Maipo, Chile

2. **Monumento Natural El Morado:** Immerse yourself in the tranquility of Monumento Natural El Morado, a protected area home to a diverse range of flora and fauna. Hike through lush forests, past cascading waterfalls, and reach the iconic Morado Glacier, a mesmerizing sight against the backdrop of the mountains.

Monumento Natural El Morado, Cajón del Maipo, Chile

3. **San Francisco Glacier Trek:** Conquer the San Francisco Glacier, one of the most accessible glaciers in the Andes Mountains. Embark on a guided trek through the glacial valley, marvel at the

towering ice formations, and witness the power of nature up close.

San Francisco Glacier Trek, Cajón del Maipo, Chile

EXPERIENCE THRILLING ADVENTURES

1. **White-Water Rafting in Maipo River:** Embark on a thrilling white-water rafting adventure along the Maipo River. Navigate through exhilarating rapids, surrounded by the stunning scenery of Cajón del Maipo, and create unforgettable memories.

WhiteWater Rafting in Maipo River, Cajón del Maipo, Chile

2. Mountain Biking Trails: Explore Cajón del Maipo's extensive network of mountain biking trails, catering to all skill levels. Ride through challenging climbs, scenic descents, and immerse yourself in the breathtaking landscapes.

Mountain Biking Trails, Cajón del Maipo, Chile

UNWIND IN NATURAL HOT SPRINGS

1. **Termas Colina:** Rejuvenate your body and mind at Termas Colina, a natural hot springs resort nestled amidst the mountains. Soak in the mineral-rich waters, indulge in spa treatments, and escape the hustle and bustle of city life.

Termas Colina, Cajón del Maipo, Chile

2. **Termas Baños Morales:** Experience the tranquility of Termas Baños Morales, a traditional hot springs resort known for its therapeutic waters. Relax in the open-air pools, surrounded by lush greenery, and enjoy the tranquility of the natural surroundings.

Termas Baños Morales, Cajón del Maipo, Chile

Cajón del Maipo is a haven for outdoor enthusiasts and nature lovers, offering a diverse range of activities that will leave you exhilarated and rejuvenated. From hiking amidst stunning scenery to experiencing thrilling adventures and relaxing in natural hot springs, Cajón del Maipo provides an unforgettable escape into the heart of the Andes Mountains.

CONCÓN: A BEACH TOWN WITH A VARIETY OF WATER SPORTS

Nestled along Chile's picturesque Pacific coastline, Concón is a vibrant beach town that beckons with its inviting waters, lively atmosphere, and abundance of water sports. Whether you're an adrenaline junkie seeking exhilarating adventures or a laid-back beach bum craving relaxation, Concón has something to offer everyone.

Embrace the Thrill of Water Sports

1. **Surfing:** Concón is a renowned surfing destination, boasting consistent waves and a welcoming surf community. Catch some waves at Playa Amarilla, a popular spot for both beginners and experienced surfers.

2. **Stand-Up Paddleboarding:** Glide effortlessly across the tranquil waters of Concón Bay on a stand-up paddleboard. Enjoy the serene surroundings and soak up the breathtaking views of the coastline.

3. **Kiteboarding:** Harness the power of the wind and soar above the waves with kiteboarding. Concón's consistent winds and ideal conditions make it a haven for kiteboarding enthusiasts.

4. **Bodyboarding:** Experience the thrill of bodyboarding as you ride the waves at Concón's beaches. This exhilarating sport is perfect for those seeking an adrenaline rush.

5. **Kayaking:** Explore the hidden coves and secluded inlets of Concón's coastline by kayak. Paddle at your own pace, immerse yourself in the natural beauty, and discover hidden gems along the way.

Indulge in Coastal Delights

1. **Fresh Seafood:** Concón's vibrant fish markets and restaurants offer an abundance of fresh seafood, caught daily by local fishermen. Savor the flavors of the sea with ceviche, empanadas de mariscos, or a hearty seafood stew.

2. **Local Cuisine:** Immerse yourself in Concón's culinary scene by sampling traditional Chilean dishes. Indulge in pastel de choclo, a savory corn pie, or try a hearty cazuela, a stew filled with meat, vegetables, and potatoes.

3. **Beachfront Bars and Cafés:** Relax and unwind at Concón's beachfront bars and cafés. Enjoy refreshing cocktails, indulge in delicious snacks, and soak up the vibrant atmosphere.

Explore Coastal Charm

1. **Concón Beach:** Stroll along Concón Beach, a popular spot for sunbathing, swimming, and enjoying the lively atmosphere. Soak up the sun, take a refreshing dip in the Pacific Ocean, or simply relax and watch the world go by.

2. **Concón Pier:** Take a leisurely stroll along Concón Pier, offering panoramic views of the coastline. Enjoy the fresh sea breeze, watch the fishing boats come and go, and admire the vibrant colors of the sunset.

3. **Parque La Foresta:** Escape to Parque La Foresta, a tranquil oasis amidst the bustling town. Stroll through the lush gardens, enjoy a picnic under the shade of trees, or simply relax and soak up the serenity.

4. **Concón Cultural Center:** Immerse yourself in Concón's cultural scene at the Concón Cultural Center. Explore art exhibitions, attend workshops, and experience the rich cultural heritage of the region.

5. **Concón Handicraft Market:** Browse the Concón Handicraft Market for unique souvenirs and handmade crafts. Discover local treasures, support local artisans, and bring home a piece of Concón's charm.

Concón is a dynamic coastal town that seamlessly blends thrilling water sports, delectable cuisine, and captivating cultural experiences. Whether you're seeking adventure, relaxation, or a taste of local culture, Concón promises an unforgettable coastal escape.

ISLA DE MAIPO: A SMALL ISLAND WITH VINEYARDS AND WINERIES

Isla de Maipo is indeed a small island located in the Maipo Valley, about 50 kilometers south of Santiago, Chile. It is known for its numerous vineyards and wineries, which produce some of the country's best wines.

Here are some of the most popular wineries on Isla de Maipo:

- **Viña Tarapacá:** This winery is known for its Cabernet Sauvignon and Chardonnay wines. It offers a variety of tours and tastings, including a horseback riding tour.

- **Cousiño Macul:** This winery is one of the oldest in Chile, dating back to 1854. It is known for its red wines, particularly its Cabernet Sauvignon.

- **Santa Ema:** This winery is known for its organic and biodynamic wines. It offers a variety of tours and tastings, including a tour of the winery's organic garden.

- **De Martino:** This winery is known for its innovative wines, such as its Carmenère-Syrah blend. It offers a variety of tours and tastings, including a tour of the winery's art gallery.

- **Terramater:** This winery is known for its sustainable practices. It offers a variety of tours and tastings, including a tour of the winery's solar panels and water recycling system.

In addition to its wineries, Isla de Maipo is also home to a number of other attractions, including:

- **Parque Nacional Río Maipo:** This national park is home to a variety of plants and animals, including the Chilean flamingo.

- **Embalse El Yeso:** This reservoir is a popular spot for swimming, fishing, and boating.

- **Termas Colina:** This hot springs resort is a great place to relax and soak in the mineral-rich waters.

If you are looking for a place to enjoy wine, food, and beautiful scenery, Isla de Maipo is a great option.

CONCLUSION

Chile is a captivating country that offers a diverse range of experiences for travelers. From the bustling city of Santiago to the serene coastal towns of Valparaíso and Viña del Mar to the breathtaking landscapes of the Andes Mountains, Chile has something to offer everyone. Whether you're seeking adventure, relaxation, or cultural enrichment, Chile is sure to leave you with unforgettable memories.

TIPS FOR PACKING UP AND GOING HOME

Packing up and going home can be a daunting task, but it doesn't have to be. Here are a few tips to help you make the process as smooth as possible:

- **Start planning early.** Don't leave packing to the last minute. Start thinking about what you need to pack a few days or even a week in advance. This will give you plenty of time to gather your belongings and avoid any last-minute stress.

- **Make a list.** Create a list of everything you need to pack. This will help you stay organized and make sure you don't forget anything important.

- **Pack light.** The less you pack, the easier it will be to carry your belongings and the less you'll have to worry about losing or damaging something. Only pack the essentials and leave behind anything you can buy at your destination or don't need for your trip.

- **Use packing cubes.** Packing cubes are a great way to keep your belongings organized and compressed. They come in a variety of sizes, so you can find the perfect ones for your needs.

- **Pack fragile items carefully.** Wrap fragile items in bubble wrap or packing paper to protect them from damage during transit.
- **Label your boxes.** Label your boxes clearly with your name and contact information. This will help you identify your belongings at your destination and make it easier for movers to transport them.
- **Clean as you go.** As you pack, take the time to clean your belongings. This will save you time and effort when you unpack at home.
- **Don't overpack your suitcase.** Leave some room in your suitcase for souvenirs and any additional items you may purchase on your trip.
- **Pack a carry-on bag with essentials.** Pack a carry-on bag with essential items such as toiletries, a change of clothes, and any important documents. This will ensure you have everything you need in case your luggage gets lost or delayed.
- **Take a break and relax.** Packing can be tiring, so take breaks as needed. Relax and enjoy the process of packing for your next adventure.

SAYING GOODBYE TO SANTIAGO

As you bid farewell to Santiago, the vibrant capital of Chile, take a moment to reflect on the unforgettable experiences you've had and the warm memories you've created. From exploring the bustling city center to hiking amidst the majestic Andes Mountains, from savoring the rich flavors of Chilean cuisine to immersing yourself in the vibrant cultural scene, Santiago has undoubtedly left an indelible mark on your heart.

As you board your flight or embark on your onward journey, carry with you the spirit of Santiago, its resilience, its passion, and its infectious energy. Let the memories of your time in this remarkable city serve as a source of inspiration and a reminder of the countless adventures that await you in the future.

Santiago, with its towering peaks, charming neighborhoods, and warm hospitality, will forever hold a special place in your heart. As you say goodbye, know that you've made a connection with this city that will forever be cherished.

APPENDIX

MAP OF SANTIAGO

LIST OF USEFUL PHRASES IN SPANISH

Greetings and Introductions

- **Hola:** Hello

- **Buenos días:** Good morning

- Buenas tardes: Good afternoon

- Buenas noches: Good evening

- ¿Cómo estás?: How are you?

- Me llamo [your name]: My name is [your name]

- Mucho gusto: Nice to meet you

- Encantado de conocerte: Nice to meet you too

Asking for Help and Directions

- ¿Hablas inglés?: Do you speak English?

- No hablo español: I don't speak Spanish

- ¿Me ayudas, por favor?: Can you help me, please?

- ¿Dónde está [place]? Where is [place]?

- ¿Cómo puedo llegar a [place]?: How can I get to [place]?

- ¿Cuánto cuesta [item]? How much does [item] cost?

- ¿Me puedes dar un recibo?: Can I have a receipt, please?

Shopping and Dining

- ¿Tienes [item]? Do you have [item]?

- ¿Cuánto cuesta [item]? How much does [item] cost?

- Quiero comprar [item]: I want to buy [item]

- ¿Dónde está el baño?: Where is the restroom?

- ¿Tiene menú en inglés?: Do you have an English menu?

- ¿Puedo pagar con tarjeta?: Can I pay with a card?

- La cuenta, por favor: The bill, please

Emergencies

- ¡Ayuda!: Help!

- Necesito ayuda: I need help

- Estoy perdido/a: I'm lost

- Llame a una ambulancia: Call an ambulance

- Llame a la policía: Call the police

- No entiendo: I don't understand

Additional Phrases

- Gracias: Thank you

- De nada: You're welcome

- Por favor: Please

- Lo siento: I'm sorry

- No hay problema: No problem

- Sí: Yes

- No: No

- Adiós: Goodbye

LIST OF EMERGENCY CONTACT NUMBERS

- Fire: 132

- Police: 133

- Mountain Rescue: 136

- Maritime Rescue: 137

- Tourist Police: 422 7670

- U.S. Embassy: (+56) 2 330 3000

These numbers are available 24 hours a day, 7 days a week.

In addition to these emergency contact numbers, it is also important to save the contact information of your hotel or accommodation, as well as the address of the nearest hospital or medical clinic. You may also want to consider downloading an emergency app for your smartphone, which can provide you with access to emergency services and other resources in case of an emergency.

Here are some additional tips for staying safe in Santiago:

- Be aware of your surroundings: Pay attention to what is going on around you and avoid walking alone in unfamiliar areas, especially at night.

- Keep your valuables safe: Don't carry large amounts of cash or valuables with you, and keep your belongings close to you at all times.

- Be cautious about using ATMs: Use ATMs in well-lit areas and avoid using them at night.

- Take taxis from reputable companies: Only use taxis from licensed companies, and make sure the taxi driver has a valid identification card.

- Trust your instincts: If something feels wrong, don't hesitate to walk away.

By following these tips, you can help to ensure your safety while traveling in Santiago.

Travel Plans

KINDS OF TRANSPORTATION:

Date:

Location:

Budget:

My Travel Planner

Personal Itinerary

PLACES TO GO

LOCAL FOODS TO TRY

REMINDER

TODAY'S LOG

6 AM	
7 AM	
8 AM	
9 AM	
10 AM	
11 AM	
12 PM	
1 PM	
2 PM	
3 PM	
4 PM	
5 PM	
6 PM	

KINDS OF TRANSPORTATION:

My Travel Planner

Personal Itinerary

Date:

Location:

Budget:

PLACES TO GO

LOCAL FOODS TO TRY

REMINDER

TODAY'S LOG

6 AM	
7 AM	
8 AM	
9 AM	
10 AM	
11 AM	
12 PM	
1 PM	
2 PM	
3 PM	
4 PM	
5 PM	
6 PM	

KINDS OF TRANSPORTATION:

Date:	
Location:	
Budget:	

My Travel Planner

Personal Itinerary

PLACES TO GO

LOCAL FOODS TO TRY

REMINDER

TODAY'S LOG

6 AM	
7 AM	
8 AM	
9 AM	
10 AM	
11 AM	
12 PM	
1 PM	
2 PM	
3 PM	
4 PM	
5 PM	
6 PM	

KINDS OF TRANSPORTATION:

Date:

Location:

Budget:

My Travel Planner

Personal Itinerary

PLACES TO GO

LOCAL FOODS TO TRY

REMINDER

TODAY'S LOG

6 AM	
7 AM	
8 AM	
9 AM	
10 AM	
11 AM	
12 PM	
1 PM	
2 PM	
3 PM	
4 PM	
5 PM	
6 PM	

KINDS OF TRANSPORTATION:

Date:

Location:

Budget:

My Travel Planner

Personal Itinerary

PLACES TO GO

LOCAL FOODS TO TRY

REMINDER

TODAY'S LOG

6 AM	
7 AM	
8 AM	
9 AM	
10 AM	
11 AM	
12 PM	
1 PM	
2 PM	
3 PM	
4 PM	
5 PM	
6 PM	

Made in the USA
Middletown, DE
14 January 2025